"Everywhere I go women are searching for discipleship tools, either for themselves or for those they are discipling. Katie Orr has delivered up a fresh, substantive tool to accomplish both. FOCUSed15 is a serious study method that is possible even for those with demanding responsibilities. This material will fit in a variety of settings and for women everywhere on their spiritual journey."

– KATHY FERGUSON LITTON, national consultant for ministry to pastors' wives, North American Mission Board

"Katie Orr brings a unique and productive method of studying Scripture to the world of Bible studies. I enthusiastically encourage women to explore this effective and enjoyable method of Bible study!"

—SUZIE HAWKINS, author and longtime member of Southern Baptist Convention Pastors' Wives, wife of O. S. Hawkins

"Katie Orr has designed devotional material for the busy woman in mind—a focused 15 minutes a day that leads the reader to encounter the biblical text with guidance that reinforces solid principles of biblical interpretation and helpful application that makes God's Word come alive in our daily choices."

—TREVIN WAX, managing editor of *The Gospel Project*, LifeWay Christian Resources

"Katie Orr has a passion for Scripture and for women to know Scripture. This passion shows in her FOCUSed15 Bible study method, which she uses to lead women through books of the Bible and topical doctrinal studies. She proves that inductive Bible study doesn't have to be complicated but can be deeply impactful and fruitful."

—CHRISTINE HOOVER, author of *From Good to Grace* and *The Church Planting Wife*

"FOCUSed15 gives women an opportunity to learn the tools of inductive Bible study in bite-sized chunks. Perfect for anyone who is committed to studying the Word in this time-crunched culture!"

—ANDREA BUCZYNSKI, vice president of global leadership development/human resources for CRU

"The Scriptures are like jewels. When you look from different angles they glimmer in beautiful and unexpected ways. FOCUSed15 gives a fresh way to examine and enjoy the most precious words on Earth. Katie Orr's zeal for God's Word is contagious and may forever change the way you engage the Bible."

—JESSE LANE, vice president of connections at Seed Company

"Katie Orr has both the unique ability to make deep, meaningful Bible study doable for others and the passion for helping women love God more through the study of His Word. Through her Bible studies, Katie teaches others how to methodically grasp and absorb biblical theology in digestible bite-sized chunks. Her distinct and approachable gift of leading others through Scripture gives those with a desire to dive into God's Word a wonderful opportunity to both understand and apply deep biblical truths in their everyday."

—CHRYSTAL EVANS HURST, coauthor *of Kingdom Woman*

"I believe weariness is a feeling, and hope is a choice to believe what God says is true really is true. But sometimes, when the storms of life hit, I forget to choose hope, and need someone to come alongside me to help me remember. In this beautiful Bible study, Katie Orr invites us into a deeper understanding of what God's Word has to say about the subject, and reconnects us with the heart of our Savior. There's nothing like diving into Scripture to give a girl hope, and Katie helps us make the leap."

—BROOKE MCGLOTHLIN, president and cofounder of Raising Boys Ministries, and coauthor of *Hope for the Weary Mom: Let God Meet You in the Mess*

EVERYDAY

faith

Drawing Near to His Presence

KATIE ORR

Other books in the
FOCUSed15 Bible study series:

Everyday Hope:
Holding Fast to His Promise

Everyday Love:
Bearing Witness to His Purpose

Everyday Peace:
Standing Firm in His Provision

EVERYDAY

faith

Drawing Near to
His Presence

KATIE ORR

NEW HOPE®
PUBLISHERS
Gospel-Centered. Missions-Driven.

BIRMINGHAM, ALABAMA

New Hope® Publishers
PO Box 12065
Birmingham, AL 35202-2065

NewHopePublishers.com
New Hope Publishers is a division of WMU®.

Library of Congress Control Number: 2015917318

Cover Designer: Michelle Drashman
Interior Designer: Glynese Northam

ISBN-10: 1-59669-461-0
ISBN-13: 978-1-59669-461-3

N164101 • 0617 • 2M4

Dedication

To my kiddos: *Kenneth, Anna,* and *Michael,*

I fervently pray you will continually choose to draw near to our
faithful, loving, gracious God in your everyday.
I love you.

Contents

Introduction

HAVING FAITH CAN feel a bit like Indiana Jones's leap onto the hidden bridge. Remember that scene in the movie *Indiana Jones and the Last Crusade*? Indy is at the end of his quest to find the Holy Grail, and finds himself at the edge of a deep ravine his instructions tell he must cross. There is no climbing down and the other side is much too far to jump. But he has been told there is a way, and that it requires faith. So he steps out . . .

Faith is the conviction of things not seen, right?

Indy takes that leap of faith and we all hold our breath while images of Harrison Ford splattered on the bottom of the canyon swirl through our head. He falls several feet, and just as we think the hope of finding the Holy Grail is forever dashed, his feet find a camouflaged bridge leading to the other side . . . and we all exhale.

This is an incredible picture of faith, but for a very long time I avoided the promptings of the Holy Spirit's call to faith-filled obedience because I thought it would end me up on an Indiana Jones cliff with an extraordinary choice of faith in front of me; one I fear I'd not be able to make. My view of living by faith equated to the extreme Christian cliff jump living that was reserved for the super spiritual; certainly unattainable by me. Yet, God has been a gentle guide, and over the years, He has shown me that faith is not primarily displayed in the cliff dwelling, monumental, do-or-die instances. Our faith is primarily proved in the everyday, mundane, one-foot-in-front-of-the-other moments.

> So let me tell you what faith is: faith is belief with legs on it.
> —ADRIAN ROGERS, *What Every Christian Ought to Know Day by Day*

Faith is the vehicle by which we experience God. He has acted, pursued, and called us to Himself, but He can't make the choice of faith for us. By His glorious grace, He has provided everything we need for eternity with Him. Salvation is a gift, faith is how we receive it. "For by grace you have been saved through faith. And this is not your own doing; it is the gift of God, not a result of works, so that no one may boast" (Ephesians 2:8–9). But it doesn't stop there. Faith is also how we experience everyday grace and how we live a godly life until we join Him in glory.

Clinging to God's grace instead of depending on our checklists for spiritual growth requires faith. Choosing to follow where He leads today instead of allowing the world to sway us requires faith. Casting our doubts aside to embrace the truths about who God is—even when our circumstances tempt us to believe otherwise—requires faith.

Opening this study requires faith, too, and I'm so excited you are here with me on this journey. Truly. I know you're busy. I imagine you have laundry waiting, important paperwork pending, and precious people who need you today. It's difficult to silence the tyranny of the urgent, yet it's through His empowering presence we receive all we need to fulfill the roles and complete the tasks He's given us (2 Peter 1:3). The pursuit of everyday faith is a worthwhile journey and a fruitful endeavor that will lead only to a greater, more intimate walk with our Lord.

You've made a good choice.

During our time together, over the next four weeks, we are going to study Hebrews 11. There are 40 verses, and we are going to dive prayerfully and intentionally into each one, using the FOCUSed15 method of study. I'll provide ways to go deeper at every turn, but I want you to feel full freedom to stick to the time you have available for that day. You truly can obtain a worthwhile study of faith in only 15 minutes a day. I also encourage you to see the daily schedule as simply a suggestion. If you want to do two days in one, go for it! If one day's study takes you three, awesome. No one's going to be checking over your shoulder to see if you are doing this "right." Sit back and enjoy God's Word, in your own way, in your own time.

As we begin our time together in Hebrews, spend a few moments asking God to do what only He can in your heart over the next four weeks. You might consider these prayers, which are inspired by truths from Psalm 119.

Where my soul is filled with sorrow,
strengthen me with Your words.

Where my heart seeks selfish gain,
turn me toward Your statutes.

When I'm afflicted and discouraged,
fill me with hope and comfort in Your promises.

Give me understanding, that I may keep Your law
and observe it with my whole heart.

Open my eyes, that I may behold wonderful things
out of Your law.

Give me a love for Your Word.
Make it my meditation all the day.

Consider writing out this prayer—or a prayer of dependency in your own words—on a 3x5 card to keep as a bookmark to this study and a reminder to begin each day's study with a dependency on God's Spirit to lead and teach.

I'm praying for you as you begin this journey toward everyday faith. God has begun a great work in you, and He will bring it to completion (Philippians 1:6)! I'm excited to walk this path of faith together in the weeks to come.

Thanks for taking this journey with me.

—Katie

The Need for FOCUS

IF THIS IS your first FOCUSed15 study, you'll want to carefully read through the following introduction and study method instructions. After that, I'll see you on Day 1!

It's hard to focus.

In a world filled with continual demands for my attention, I struggle to keep a train of thought. Tasks I need to do. Appointments I need to remember. Projects I need to complete.

Yeah, it's hard to focus.

Without a good focus for my days, I wander. I lack the ability to choose well and avoid the tyranny of the urgent. Without focus, days become a blur—tossed back and forth between the pressing and the enticing.

WHY FOCUS MATTERS

I felt pretty lost during my first attempts at spending time with God in the Bible. After a few weeks of wandering around the Psalms and flipping through the New Testament, I realized I had no clue what I was doing.

It felt like a pretty big waste of time.

I knew the Bible was full of life-changing truths and life-giving promises, but I needed to learn how to focus on the details to see all that Scripture held for me.

In the medical world, we depend on the microscope. Even with all the fancy machines that can give test results in seconds, the microscope has yet to become obsolete. Some things can only be discovered through the lens of the scope.

What looks like nothing to the naked eye is actually teeming with life-threatening bacteria. Even under the microscope they may not be seen at first glance. But with the smallest adjustment of the focus, the blurry cloud of the field in view is brought into focus and the finest details are revealed.

And those details matter.

You need a microscope to make a diagnosis, but the microscope itself doesn't make the discoveries. It takes a trained eye to distinguish between cells. The average person may be able to figure out how to use the microscope to find a cell and get it in focus, but without training, the beginner will not know the clinical significance of what is seen.

Similarly, when we approach God's Word, we must learn to focus on what we are seeing and develop a trained eye to know its significance.

READY FOR MORE

I grew up in a shallow Christian culture. Don't do drugs. Don't have sex. Don't tell lies. Read your Bible. Be a light—sold-out for Jesus. This was the sum of being a good Christian, or so I thought.

Now, I'm your typical firstborn list-checker, so the do's and don'ts worked for me . . . for a while. But as I got older and the temptations of the don'ts became more enticing, I began to wonder if this Christianity thing was worth it.

Is this really what people spend their lives chasing? Seems tiring—and ultimately worthless.

Yet, God was drawing my heart—I could undeniably feel it—but I knew I was missing something. I thought I'd check out this reading-the-

Bible thing. Sure, I had read a devotional or two and knew all the Bible stories, but I didn't feel I knew God Himself.

A bit nervous, I drove to the local bookstore to buy my first really nice Bible. I excitedly drove back home, and headed straight to my room, opened up my leather-bound beauty and began to read . . .

. . . and nothing happened.

I'm not quite sure what I was expecting, but it sure wasn't confusion and frustration. I decided to give it another try the next day and still heard nothing. I had no clue what I was reading.

In all my years of storing up the do's and don'ts in my how-to-be-a-good-Christian box, I never caught a *how* or *why*.

For years I stumbled through my black leather Bible with very little learned on the other side of it all. Yet, God was faithful to lead and speak, and I fully believe that He can and does speak to us through His Word, even if we are as clueless as I was.

However, I also believe that God's Word is meant to be a great catalyst in our growth, and as we pursue how to better know God through His Word, we will experience Him in deeper ways.

You and I need a healthy, rich diet of God's Word in order to grow. And as we read, study, and learn to digest the Bible, we move toward becoming more like Christ. When we pursue the nearness of God, the don'ts become lackluster compared to the life-giving promises of His Word.

A FOCUSed 15 MINUTES

Over time, I learned incredible Bible study tools that took my time with God in His Word to a deeper level. Yet with each method, Bible study seemed to take more and more time. Certain seasons of life allow for a leisurely time in the Bible; my experience has proven that most of my days don't.

but oftentimes devotionals, study Bibles, and the latest, greatest Bible teacher can be a crutch that keeps us from learning how to walk intimately with God on our own. While I do believe there is only one true meaning of each verse, God has a personalized word to speak to each of us through this study. Receiving big news from a loved one in a deliberate and personalized way means so much more to us than receiving the news third-hand, and when the Holy Spirit reveals a message to our hearts through God's Word, it will be something we hold to much more closely than someone else's experience of God. If at the end of the week, you are still unsure of the meaning of the passage, you will have time to look through commentaries.

For a list of my favorite online and print resources, including Greek study tools, commentaries, cross-referencing tools, and study Bibles, check out my resources page at KatieOrr.me.

How to FOCUS

OVER THE NEXT four weeks we will study faith together using the FOCUSed15 study method. Think of me as your Bible coach. I will point you to the goal, give you what you need, and cheer you on—but you'll be the one doing the work.

The FOCUSed15 method may be different than other studies you've completed. We're focusing on quality, not quantity. The goal is not to see how quickly we can get through each verse, but how deeply we can go into each verse and find everything we can about the faith portrayed. This is how we can go deeper, in as little as 15 minutes a day, by looking at the same passage over the course of several days, each day using a new lens to view it. We're not trying to get everything we can out of the passage the first time we sit in front of it. Instead, we'll come back to it again and again, peeling back each layer, 15 minutes at a time.

Here is where we're headed:

- Week 1—Preparing to FOCUS
- Week 2—FOCUSing on Hebrews 11:1–12
- Week 3—FOCUSing on Hebrews 11:13–28
- Week 4—FOCUSing on Hebrews 11:29–40

THE FOCUSed15 BIBLE STUDY METHOD

For me, high school history homework typically consisted of answering a set of questions at the end of the chapter. I quickly found that the best use of my time was to take each question, one at a time, and skim through the chapter with the question in mind. So, if the question was about Constantine, I would read the chapter wearing my "Constantine Glasses." All I looked for were facts about Constantine.

Little did I know then, this "glasses" method would become my favorite way to study God's Word. The FOCUSed15 method is essentially changing to a new pair of glasses with each read, using a different focus than the read before. Together, we will study one passage for five days, each day using a different part of the FOCUSed15 method.

- Day 1—Foundation: Enjoy Every Word
- Day 2—Observation: Look at the Details
- Day 3—Clarification: Uncover the Original Meaning
- Day 4—Utilization: Discover the Connections
- Day 5—Summation: Respond to God's Word

For each day in our study, I will guide you through a different lens of the FOCUSed15 study method, designed to be completed in as little as 15 minutes a day. There are also bonus study ideas with every day, providing ways to spend more time and dig even deeper if you can. We'll also pray together each day, declaring our dependence on the Spirit of God to open the eyes of our hearts to the truths in God's Word.

FOUNDATION
Enjoy Every Word

Many of us are conditioned to read through Scripture quickly and are often left having no idea what we just read. So, to kick off our studies, we will write out our verses. Nothing too fancy, but an incredibly efficient way to slow down and pay attention to each word on the page.

OBSERVATION

Look at the Details

With our foundation work behind us, we'll spend the next day looking for truths in God's Word. This is a powerful use of our time; we cannot rightly apply the Bible to our lives if we do not accurately see what is there. Observation is simply noting what we see by asking ourselves "What is true here?" We're not yet trying to figure out what it means, we are simply beginning an assessment. I will guide you along the way as we look for specific truths like, "What does this passage say is true about my hope?" or "What is true about God in this passage?"

CLARIFICATION

Uncover the Original Meaning

This is going to be fun. We are going to look at the original language of the verses. Our three passages are in the New Testament, so we will be looking up the Greek. To do this we will follow three simple steps:

Step 1: DECIDE which English word to study.
In this step, we will look for any repeated or keywords to look up, then choose one to learn more about.

Step 2: DISCOVER the Greek word in an interlinear Bible.
Next, using an interlinear Bible, we'll find the original Greek word for the word we chose in Step 1.

Step 3: DEFINE the Greek word using a Greek lexicon.
Finally, we will learn about the full meaning of each Greek word using a Greek lexicon, which is very much like a dictionary.

We'll walk through an example together each week. You can also book-mark How to Do a Greek Word Study in the appendix for you to reference throughout the study.

UTILIZATION
Discover the Connections

> The infallible rule of interpretation of Scripture is the Scripture itself: and therefore, when there is a question about the true and full sense of any Scripture . . . it must be searched and known by other places that speak more clearly.
>
> —*The Westminster Confession of Faith*

Ever notice the little numbers and letters inserted in your study Bible? Most have them. The numbers are footnotes, helpful bits of information about the original text. The little letters are cross-references and important tools for study.

Cross-references are doing just that, referencing across the Bible where the word or phrase is used in other passages. They may also refer to a historical event or prophecy significant to the verse you are studying.

Together, we will follow a few of the cross-references for each of our passages, as they will often lead us to a better understanding of the main teaching of our verses. If your Bible doesn't have cross-references, no worries! I will provide verses for you to look up, and refer you to online tools for bonus studies.

SUMMATION

Respond to God's Word

> A respectable acquaintance with the opinions of the giants of the past, might have saved many an erratic thinker from wild interpretations and outrageous inferences.
>
> —CHARLES SPURGEON

This is when we begin to answer the question "How should this passage affect me?" To do this we will do three things:

1. IDENTIFY—Find the main idea of the passage.

With a robust study of our passage accomplished, we can now do the work of interpretation. Interpretation is simply figuring out what it all means. This is oftentimes difficult to do. However, if we keep in mind the context and make good observations of the text, a solid interpretation will typically result.

This day is when we will finally consult our study Bibles and commentaries! Commentaries are invaluable tools when interpreting Scripture. They are available on the entire Bible, as well as volumes on just one book of the Bible. For a list of free online commentaries, as well as in-print investments, check out KatieOrr.me/Resources.

2. MODIFY—Evaluate my beliefs in light of the main idea.

Once we have figured out what the passage means, we can now apply the passage to our lives. Many tend to look at application as simply finding something to change in their actions. Much in the Bible will certainly lead us to lifestyle changes, but there is another category of application that we often miss: what we believe.

We must learn to see the character of God in what we study and ask ourselves how our view of Him lines up with what we see. Of course it is helpful to look for do's and don'ts to follow, but without an ever-growing knowledge of who God is, the commands become burdensome.

3. GLORIFY—Align my life to reflect the truth of God's Word.

When we see God for the glorious, grace-filled Savior He is, the natural response is worship; the do's and don'ts become a joy as they become a way to honor the One we love with our lives. Worship is true application.

ALL OF THIS . . . IN 15 MINUTES?!

Yes, I know this seems like a lot of ground to cover. Don't worry! I will be here to walk you through each day. Remember, instead of trying to go as fast as we can through a passage, we are going to take it slow and intentional. We'll look at one passage for an entire week, and apply one part of the method to the passage each day.

THE CHEAT SHEET

At the end of most days' studies, I've included a "cheat sheet." While trying to complete a Bible study, I've often been paralyzed with wondering, "Am I doing this the right way?" The cheat sheet is there for you to use as a reference point. It is not a list of correct answers, however, and is meant instead to provide just a little bit of guidance here and there to let you know you are on the right track.

There are also several references in the appendix you may want to refer to throughout our time together. If you are new to Bible study, you might consider spending a day to read through the appendices before beginning your study. I hope those pages will be of great help to you.

A NOTE TO THE OVERWHELMED

Bible study is not a competition or something to achieve. It is a way of communicating with our magnificent God. If you have little time or mental capacity (I've been there, moms with little ones!), ignore the bonus study ideas and enjoy what you can. Keep moving through the study each day, and know that you have taken a step of obedience to meet with God in His Word. Other seasons of life will allow for longer, deeper study. For now, embrace these precious moments in the Word and remember that Jesus is your righteousness. When God looks at you—overwhelmed and burned-out though you are—He sees the faithful obedience and perfection of Christ on your behalf, and He is pleased. Rest in that today, weary one.

PREPARING TO **FOCUS**

What Is Biblical Faith?

Introduction to Hebrews 11

PREPARING TO **FOCUS**

I'M A SUCKER for a good TV series. So is my husband. If the two of us are both interested in a show—and it's available on Netflix—look out! Though we have been known to stay up until 4 a.m. on a Friday evening (in our pre-kiddo days) just to finish off an intriguing season, one thing you will never find us doing is starting a show in the middle of a series. Never ever.

Picking up a novel to start reading from page 178 is absurd. Walking into the middle of a good TV series or movie is just silly. You miss all the previous character development and storyline. Without having taken the journey through the previous scenes, the implications of words said and actions taken by the characters are lost, and potentially misunderstood.

Though it may seem to some a disjointed collection of words, the Bible is actually quite a masterpiece. The more I study it, the more I realize the depths of cohesion each book of the Bible has with one another. There are threads that weave in and out of both the Old and New Testaments, and every verse, every word is there with great purpose. There are no throw away passages.

Yet, early on in my journey with Christ, most of the biblical themes were lost on me; for years my experience of Bible study was like reading a disjointed storyline. I felt as if I was starting a book from the wrong page.

So, to begin our study, this week we will look at the "book-ends" of Hebrews 11, to help us understand the storyline moving up to this chapter and get a better context for the truths embedded in this familiar "Hall of Faith" passage. After that, we will study Hebrews 11 verse-by-verse over the course of three weeks.

Obviously, we don't have time to read through the entire Bible today. However, there are a few simple ways for us to get some sort of idea of what is going on in the Book of Hebrews and how it relates to the rest of the story of the Bible. This week's study will do just that: find our place in the biblical story. (If you are new to the Bible, consider reading the first few items in the appendix to help get a big picture of the Bible and its contents.)

1. To start our study, read all of Hebrews 11. Just sit back and enjoy it. Don't try to figure it all out, but don't tune out either. Read with purpose to understand what the big picture of the chapter looks like. As you read, note every instance of the word faith. You might consider underlining, circling, or highlighting the word faith every time you see it.

2. What words and/or phrases catch your attention from your initial read of Hebrews 11?

Jesus' life, death, and Resurrection changed everything for us, and the author of Hebrews spends much time on this work of Christ on our

behalf. Jesus is often referred to as "superior" in Hebrews.
He is better than the angels and brings a better hope. Jesus is the guarantee and mediator of a better covenant with God. Christ became the great high priest who eliminated our need for the temple, the Law, and a priest to enter into the holy of holies on our behalf.

The implications of this new and living way Jesus provided for us was not lost on the original audience, the Jewish Christians who received this letter. They knew their Hebrew religion well. Many of them either formerly practiced the Old Testament law, or remembered family who did. Sacrifice after sacrifice was offered by the high priest on behalf of their sins. Law after law was observed. Yet none of it was enough to satisfy the debt owed by their sins. Until Jesus.

> But we see him who for a little while was made lower than the angels, namely Jesus, crowned with glory and honor because of the suffering of death, so that by the grace of God he might taste death for everyone.
>
> — HEBREWS 2:9

(If you are unfamiliar with the Old Testament and the laws the Hebrews had to adhere to, take some time to read through the section on the Old Testament Law in the appendix.)

Our Savior is supreme. His work on the Cross is complete. Through Christ we are granted new life, access to a holy God, and given everything we need to walk intimately with God. The Law is no longer. The requisite sacrifice for sin is satisfied. Because of Christ's righteous works on our behalf, you and I now need for nothing—but faith.

Receiving Christ's work by faith is the only part you and I play in salvation. Placing my faith in God's providing character, guiding Spirit, and powerful Word is the only accelerator I can add to the process of becoming more like Jesus. And faith is the only lasting fuel that will keep me clinging to Christ.

Every pursuit I attempt without faith in Jesus is a plan that will inevitably fail.

> God, reveal the places where I am clinging more to my plans than Your provision. Open my eyes to clearly see the sufficiency and supremacy of Christ's sacrifice for my sins. Show me what it looks like to live in the day-by-day faith of all Christ has done for me, and all that is promised to come. Thank You for your provision.

⁔ BONUS STUDY ⁔

If you are ready for an even deeper study this first week, check out this bonus study section at the end of each day. It will take you through a quick read of the Book of Hebrews over the week.

Read the background on Hebrews to learn more about the book. If you own a study Bible, this information is easily accessed right before the Book of Hebrews begins. There are also many great (free!) online websites that can help you in your search. (Check out KatieOrr.me/Resources for current links to free online websites.) You can also check the cheat sheet if you get stuck, or are short on time today.

Jot down anything new or of interest from your background search, then note the following essentials of the Book of Hebrews:

Author (Who wrote the Book of Hebrews?)

Audience (To whom was this book written, and when?)

Aim (Why was Hebrews written?)

Read Hebrews 1–2, looking for what is true about Christ. Note what you learn.

BONUS STUDY CHEAT SHEET

The Essentials of Hebrews

Author: Debated/unknown

Audience:

• Most likely written before AD 70 (the destruction of the temple), circa AD 64–68.

• Written to second generation Christians.

• Written to a Hebrew Christian audience.

Aim:

• Probably a letter (epistle) written to a church.

• Written as encouragement amidst persecution.

• Shows that Christ is preeminent—greater than all.

• Shows that faith in Jesus is greater than the Law.

FOCUSing on Hebrews 10:19–25

PREPARING TO **FOCUS**

If God doesn't rule your mundane, then he doesn't rule
you. Because that is where you live.

—*Paul Tripp*

THE BIBLE HAS much to say about faith, and God's Word is meant to be
studied. We all know that! But the Bible is also meant to change us. Our
churches (even some of our seminaries) are filled with men and women
who know a lot about Jesus. They have a great knowledge of the Bible,
but there is a chasm between what they learn and what they look like.

If I'm honest, there are plenty of days my life looks as if I've never
read the Bible. Because, it's easy to forget what I've encountered through
God's Word. And when I live this forgetful life, I deny by my lifestyle the
very faith I claim to have.

"For if anyone is a hearer of the word and not a doer, he is like a man
who looks intently at his natural face in a mirror. For he looks at himself
and goes away and at once forgets what he was like" (James 1:23–24).

1. Spend a few moments in prayer, asking God to sear the truths of the gospel
onto your heart in an unforgettable, life-changing way.

2. Take a peek at the section headings in your Bible throughout Hebrews. As

you come across any headings in the Book of Hebrews that talk of the character of Christ, jot them below. If your Bible doesn't have headings, simply do a quick scan of each chapter and look for any repeated words that stand out to you.

If you don't have time to read all of Hebrews, taking a glance at the headings that come before this passage gives a quick way to grab insight of the main points the author has made. This is a great habit to practice whenever you come to a passage or verse tucked away in a book you are unfamiliar with.

If you were to read the entire book, you might have noticed a repeated word: *therefore*. This nine-letter word is one of the most powerful words in the Bible, and whenever you read it, it should trigger the question, "What is the *therefore* there for?" Cheesy, I know, but it's catchy and since I was first taught this simple little Bible study trick, it has been a trigger for many exciting studies.

In today's passage, we encounter a therefore. In fact, there are over 20 uses of the word *therefore* in the Book of Hebrews. The writer laid foundation upon foundation of truths about Jesus and the implications of those truths. From Hebrews 4:14 through 10:18, the author made a case for the foundation of our faith. Over and over, the author pointed to the work of Christ and how Jesus fulfilled the demands of the Old Testament Law, and then provided a great summary statement in 10:19–21.

3. Read this summary statement (Hebrews 10:19–21) and write it below:

These verses are chock-full of truths about who we are because of all that Christ has done for us.

4. Now read Hebrews 10:22–25 and list out the commands we are given.

Faith. Hope. Love. This is what the therefore is there for. To propel us into a fully assured faith that confidently moves into the nearness of our Holy God, to encourage us to cling to our steadfast anchor of hope we have through the gospel of Jesus, and to follow in the footsteps of our Savior who sacrificially loved others.

We were not rescued from our sin simply for our own good. God's grace certainly brought us great good; however, we were saved with great purpose. You and I are on this earth for a reason, to live out our faith and continue the work of Christ who brings many sons to glory (Hebrews 2:10). We are living in the therefore. God has saved me. God has saved you.

Therefore: Draw near. Hold fast. Bear witness.

> *God, help us to live in the therefore. Not out of guilt or duty, but out of an overflowing adoration of who You are. Holy Spirit, stir up in us a deep desire to draw nearer to You with every passing moment. Thank You Jesus, for all You have done for us so that we can be called heirs of God.*

⸬ BONUS STUDY ⸬

Read Hebrews 3–5, looking for what is true about Christ. Note what you learn.

CHEAT SHEET

2. Headings in Hebrews that point to the character of Christ:

The Supremacy of God's Son

Jesus Greater Than Moses

Jesus the Great High Priest

The Certainty of God's Promise

Jesus Compared to Melchizedek

Jesus, High Priest of a Better Covenant

Redemption Through the Blood of Christ

Christ's Sacrifice Once for All

(Headings will vary from Bible to Bible. These are from the *ESV Study Bible*.)

4. Read Hebrews 10:19–25 and list out the commands:

Let us draw near in full assurance of faith (v. 22)

Let us hold fast to our hope (v. 23)

Let us consider how to stir up one another to love and good works (v. 24)

FOCUSing on Hebrews 12:1–2

PREPARING TO **FOCUS**

The human heart takes good things like a successful career, love, material possessions, even family, and turns them into ultimate things. Our hearts deify them as the center of our lives, because, we think, they can give us significance and security, safety and fulfillment, if we attain them.

—TIM KELLER, *Counterfeit Gods: The Empty Promises of Money, Sex, and Power, and the Only Power that Matters*

MY HOUSE IS overflowing. The shoes bins are stuffed to the brim, most of my drawers won't shut all the way without a bit of finessing, and there is a daily battle in my closet for clothes hangers. There are all-too-many cabinet drawers, which have succumbed to the title "junk drawer," and our one-car garage is one big gathering place for everything but a car. Yet, the clutter isn't confined to my house. Every few weeks I have to spend time deleting images and videos from my phone because it's bogged down with the sheer volume of family memories I long to capture for future enjoyment. And I can't just dump them all to my computer because it's out of space as well.

Some days I feel stuck in the sludge of mail to sort, laundry baskets of odds and ends that need a home, and a computer that needs extra time to get to work. The physical and electronic clutter slows down my everyday rhythm and keeps me from moving forward.

Even if you boast a home of neatness and simplicity, or the newest phone with tons of storage, you face clutter too. Our lives are filled to the brim with activities, apps, and achievements that can prove to be great distractions from our true purpose in life; they keep us from intimacy with God.

Today's passage may be a familiar one to you, and one that is often looked at as a command to keep away from sin. It certainly includes an exhortation to remove the sin from our lives, but there is much more in these words we need to pay attention to. We will begin to define faith today. If faith is not primarily proven in the Indiana Jones moments, but instead in our moment-by-moment, then what does it look like?

1. Open today's time in the Word by journaling a brief prayer in the space below, asking God to open your eyes to the truths in Hebrews 12:1–2.

These verses contain a conclusion statement for the examples of faith we will study in Hebrews 11, beginning with another *therefore*. The author of Hebrews has gone to great lengths to record heroes of the faith for us to look to. These were men and women who understood what it meant to live a life of faith, and we are to learn from their examples.

"Therefore . . . let us also" (Hebrews 12:1).

2. Read Hebrews 12:1–2 and record below all the commands the author tells us to do:

Every weight. Every sin. These two are not necessarily the same. Just like the cherished images of my little ones can bog down my phone, we too can be hindered in unlikely ways: The pursuit of good grades or a promotion at work. Attempting to keep our children, parents, neighbors, boss, or (fill-in-the-blank) happy. Facebook, Candy Crush, or *Downton Abbey*. The seemingly harmless, even good, everyday gifts and responsibilities can rob energy from our journey toward intimacy with God.

> The fight of faith—the race of the Christian life—is not fought well or run well by asking, "what's wrong with this or that?" but by asking, "is it in the way of greater faith and greater love and greater purity and greater courage and greater humility and greater patience and greater self-control?" Not: "Is it a sin?" But: "Does it help me run? Is it in the way?"
>
> —JOHN PIPER, from his sermon,
> *"Running with the Witnesses"*

The men and women we will study in the weeks to come were heroes, but they were also ordinary people. Ordinary people God chose to do extraordinary things through, by their everyday choices of running the race of faith well. As we will see more in tomorrow's study, faith is the coming—the drawing near—to God. And if faith is drawing near to God, we must fight to remove anything that keeps us from His presence.

Even the good things.

> What does it mean to have other gods? . . . It means turn-
> ing a good thing into an ultimate thing.
>
> —TIM KELLER, *Every Good Endeavour:*
> *Connecting Your Work to God's Work*

3. *Every weight*. Spend some extended time today journaling, asking God to reveal to you the good things in your life that have become a distraction and hurdle from running the race toward intimacy with God.

4. *Every sin*. Now take a few moments to take an honest look at your every-day, and the sin that clings closely. Likely culprits are anger, envy, pride, or selfishness. I struggle daily with many of these. If you have additional time left today, read Ephesians 4:20–32 and continue in confession of the sinful patterns you need to throw away, so that you can pursue God more fully today.

Every choice we face is an opportunity to show faith by drawing near. When I am wronged and wounded and want to lash out, I have two potential paths to follow. I can choose anger, resentment, and retaliation, or I can relinquish my desires for justice and all I believe I'm entitled to, and choose faith. Draw near to God through the obedience to His way. Forgiveness. Mercy. Grace. It takes great faith to deny my selfish desires and follow the example of Christ.

But when I choose God's way—the way proclaimed in His Word, modeled by Christ, and enabled by the Spirit within me—I draw near in that choice and I say with my actions that God is good, God knows best, and the nearness of God is what I truly want.

Whether it is the closely clinging sin in our lives, or the innocent yet increasing distractions, faith is throwing away everything that gets in the way of drawing near to God.

God, I need You. I am continually in conflict with my sin nature and the distractions of my days. I want to live in the nearness of You. Enable me, Holy Spirit, to lay aside everything that hinders my relationship with You. Meet me in my mess, Father, and renew my desires to be close to You.

⸎ BONUS STUDY ⸎

Read Hebrews 6–8, looking for what is true about Christ. Note what you learn.

CHEAT SHEET

2. Commands in Hebrews 12:1–2:

Lay aside every weight.

Lay aside every sin which clings closely to us.

Run with endurance the race set before us.

Look to Jesus as you run.

FOCUSing on Hebrews 4:16; 7:25; and 10:1

PREPARING TO **FOCUS**

WE WILL BE spending much time together in the weeks to come looking back on the "heroes" of our faith—men and women the author of
Hebrews chose to highlight from the Old Testament. Remember, Hebrews
was written as a letter, and the people listed in this "Hall of Faith" are individuals the original recipients of Hebrews would have been familiar with.

While there is much we can and will learn from the faith-filled actions
of these people, it is important to remember that these "heroes" were not
always heroic! There are just as many (if not more) instances where they
made wrong choices, walked in fear, and chose their own comfort and
desires over the presence of God.

Truth is, there are moments in my own past (and probably more to
come) that are not quickly forgotten. I've had seasons of heart rebellion
I wish were not on my timeline. Decisions made that I'd like to declare a
do-over. We all have moments of deep regret. Dark secrets we hope never
come to light. Disobedience we'd rather not make public. Our tendency
is to keep these blemishes hidden—even from God. Just as the first man
and woman hid from their Maker the moment after their first betrayal,
we too have a run-and-hide mentality when it comes to our failures.

On Day 2, we studied an incredible truth in Hebrews 10. Remember
what the therefore was there for? Generation after generation attempted
to live up to God's holy standard. Generation after generation failed.

Miserably. But God sent His Son, Jesus, and everything changed. The veil that separated us from the holy presence of God was torn in two, and we have been granted access to the very presence of God, which demands perfection. (If you are unfamiliar with the Old Testament Law and the sacrificial system these generations had to follow, refer to Understanding the Old Testament Ceremonial Law in the appendix for more information.)

No man or woman who has walked this earth has lived a life of perfect faith—except Jesus, our ultimate hero and example of faith. Jesus' perfect life and sufficient sacrifice opened up a "new and living way" in which we can draw near to God in confidence, with full assurance that condemnation is no longer near. In Christ, you and I have been washed clean of all our sin.

Because of this, you and I can stand among these Hebrews 11 heroes, imperfect but journeying toward an intimate relationship with Christ. By faith, you and I can have Hall-of-Faith-worthy moments as we imitate our Savior, live by His grace, and choose to draw near to Him by faith.

1. Begin today's study in a short prayer, asking God to reveal to you more about what day-to-day faith looks like.

In yesterday's passage, we observed three commands:
- Lay aside the sin and weights that hinder our nearness to God.
- Run with endurance the race set before us.
- Look to Jesus.

Today, let's take a deeper look at one aspect of running the race of faith with endurance.

2. Look up and read Hebrews 11:1 and 11:6 again. As you read, ask yourself the question, "What does this verse teach about faith?" Record below all you learn about faith.

TRUTHS ABOUT FAITH

Did you catch the "draw near" phrase in verse 6? (Your version may say, "come to God" or "approach.") This is the same phrase used in the command given in Hebrews 10:22. In fact, there are three additional uses (all in Hebrews) of this idea of drawing near.

3. Look up Hebrews 4:16; 7:25; and 10:1. Note anything you learn about drawing near.

TRUTHS ABOUT DRAWING NEAR

Though Christ has made a way for me to approach the presence of God, I often don't experience a nearness to God. Honestly, the thought of drawing near to the presence of a holy God is often frightening. "What if He knows? What if He rejects me? What if I've gone too far?" And so, it's in this moment I must have enduring faith. I must choose to believe that—even in my darkest moments and most disobedient action—I can draw near.

Great faith is displayed in the drawing near when I want to run the other way.

4. To close today's study, look up Romans 8:1 and write it out. Spend a few quiet moments in thanksgiving for the ability to draw near to the holy presence of God. As hidden places of shame come to mind, remember that your sin is already forgiven. Choose to believe it. Confess any specific sins brought to mind. Thank God for His forgiveness. Draw near in faith. Walk forward in confidence that, in Christ, there is no condemnation.

God, I praise You that there is no condemnation for those who are in Christ Jesus. I thank You for providing the perfect sacrifice, Jesus, so that I can approach the throne of grace with confidence in Your acceptance of me. I am now adopted as Your daughter, an heir with Christ, with every spiritual blessing, and all that I need to live a godly life. Forgive me for the ways I continually mess up. Enable me, Holy Spirit, to draw near to God's mercy. Make the truths of Your Word sink deep down into my heart and recall them to mind when I need to believe them most.

.⊱. BONUS STUDY .⊱.

Read Hebrews 9–10, looking for what is true about Christ. Note what you learn.

CHEAT SHEET

2. Look up and read Hebrews 11:1 and 11:6 again. As you read, ask yourself the question, "What does this verse teach about faith?" Record below all you learn about faith.

TRUTHS ABOUT FAITH
Assurance of things hoped for. (11:1)
Conviction of things not seen. (11:1)
Without faith it is impossible to please God. (11:6)
Faith is needed to draw near to God. (11:6)
Faith that God exists. (11:6)
Faith that He rewards. (11:6)

3. Look up Hebrews 4:16; 7:25; and 10:1. Note anything you learn about drawing near.

TRUTHS ABOUT DRAWING NEAR
We are to draw near with confidence. (4:16)
We are to draw near to the throne of grace. (4:16)
We receive mercy and find grace to help in time of need when we draw near. (4:16)
Jesus is able to save those who draw near to God. (7:25)
Others tried to draw near before Christ, through the sacrifices of the law. (10:1)
Those sacrifices could not take away the sins of those who drew near. (10:1)

FOCUSing on Hebrews 12:1-2

PREPARING TO FOCUS

Faith should be first. After faith is preached, then we should teach good works. It is faith—*without* good works and *prior* to good works—that takes us to heaven. We come to God through faith alone.

—Martin Luther

WE TEND TO think of faith in terms of actions, of the do's and don'ts. Choose this, in faith. Don't do that, in faith. Give, in faith. But as we've seen this week, faith is required for something much more significant and, at times, much more difficult: drawing near.

Faith is believing that God has declared me righteous, even when I yell at my kids or disrespect my husband. Faith is turning from the sin that entangles me, in full assurance that I will find mercy and grace, and turning toward a greater dependence on the enabling power of the Holy Spirit to choose better next time. Faith is good preaching. It tells my heart what my mind knows to be true: I am loved. Fully accepted. Righteous before God. Even in my darkest of moments and seasons of rebellion.

Faith is the assurance of things hoped for. The knowledge of what the future holds fuels my faith. If I believe that what's ahead for me is abandonment or punishment, I will not draw near to God. And so faith comes in, preaches the gospel—the good news about Jesus and how that has changed me—and chooses to draw near, with the expectation of good things from a good God. Faith is looking to Jesus, clinging to all He has done in my life, all He is on my behalf, and the promises of all He will continue to do in me until my time on earth is over.

He is at work in you and me. Let's have faith in all that is to come.

> Strengthen me to give Thee no rest until Christ shall reign supreme within me in every thought, word, and deed, in a faith that purifies the heart, overcomes the world, works by love, fastens me to thee, and ever clings to the cross.
>
> —"Meeting God," *The Valley of Vision:*
> *a Collection of Puritan Prayers and Devotions*

1. Spend some time in thankful prayer. Praise God for the gracious Savior He is. Thank Him for the reality that even if we don't have this faith-thing all figured out, He is pleased with you, because Christ lived the perfect life of faith on your behalf. Praise Him for this truth!

We've covered a lot of ground this week. I hope you've found this week encouraging in your journey toward understanding what it means to life by faith. As I mentioned on Day 1, it's important that we first take the time to get a feeling for where we are in the story before we dive deep into Hebrews 11. Though I know we've only dipped our toes in the depths of truths about faith, I pray you are stepping closer to a better understanding of what faith is and what it's not.

Here's where we've been so far:

Day 1: Jesus changed everything! He opened up a new and living way for each of us to walk into through faith.

Day 2: We live in the therefore. Since Jesus has rescued us from eternity without the nearness of God, we live a life of worship. A life characterized by faith, hope, and love.

Day 3: Day-to-day faith is casting away everything, even the good or neutral, that gets in the way of drawing near to God.

Day 4: Day-to-day faith is drawing near with endurance when you feel like you should be fleeing.

2. Turn back to Hebrews 12, and read verses 1–2. List out all that is true about Jesus according to verse 2.

The last command given by the author of Hebrews is to look to Jesus. Lay aside, run with endurance, and look to Jesus. Let's take a deeper look at the Jesus we are to fix our eyes on.

3. What do you think it means that Jesus is the founder/author/ initiator of your faith? (If you have additional time today, and are familiar with how to do a Greek word study, look up the Greek word for *founder/author/ initiator*. Note what you learn. If you are not sure how to look up the Greek word, you can check it out in the cheat sheet. We'll go into depth next week on how to look up the original language on your own.)

4. Now think about Jesus as your *perfecter*. What do you think it means that Jesus is the perfecter of your faith? (Again, if you have time and inclination, look up the Greek word for *perfecter,* and note what you learn below.)

5. Read Philippians 1:6. Paul is writing an encouragement to his Christian brothers and sisters, and tells them he is "sure of this." Write out Philippians 1:6 below, and pay attention to what Paul is so certain of.

Try as I may, I cannot bring about life change. Neither can you. Without the work of Christ, there is nothing good in me. Jesus is the only good one. Without Him, I cannot walk a life of faith. He has begun a work of faith in me, He is continuing that work today, and He will complete that work until His eternal purposes come to pass. As I come to grips with the reality of Jesus as the author and perfecter of my faith, I can rest in His work in me and quit trying to make myself something I am not.

Displaying faith is not about proving myself good. Faith displayed is proof that I know a good God! Faith is a natural by-product of fixing my eyes on Jesus.

Jesus, I am so thankful that You are doing a good work in me. A work I can never do on my own. Help me to let go of my attempts to become a good person, and instead cling to the nearness of You. As I fix my eyes on You, and relentlessly pursue Your presence, grow the seed of faith inside of me that always seems too small. I praise You for Your grace, by which I have all I need to live the life You've called me to. Be glorified, even in my inkling of faith.

⁖ BONUS STUDY ⁖

Read Hebrews 11–13, looking for what is true about Christ. Note what you learn.

CHEAT SHEET

2. Truths about Jesus:

The founder of my faith.

The perfecter of my faith.

Endured the Cross.

Had a joy set before Him, which fueled Him to endure the Cross.

Despised the shame.

Is now seated at the right hand of the throne of God.

3. Founder, *archēgos*

• Definition: beginning, head, chief, ruler

• Times used: 4

• Part of speech: adjective, can also be translated as a masculine noun in reference to a prince or ruler

• Other ways it is translated: author, leader, captain

• Any special notes: Strong's #747 "one that takes the lead in any thing and thus affords an example, a predecessor in a matter, pioneer."

4. Perfecter, *teleiōtēs*

• Definition: perfecter, one who completes

• Times used: 1

• Part of speech: noun

• Other ways it is translated: finisher

• Any special notes: Strong's #5051 "one who has in his own person raised faith to its perfection and so set before us the highest example of faith."

FOCUSING ON **HEBREWS 11:1–12**

The Promise in Drawing Near

Foundation

FOCUSing ON HEBREWS 11:1–12

Hebrews 11 is known as the Hall of Faith. It's a sampling of those who have gone before us and have shown great faith. Yet, it's not recorded to merely praise the names of the individuals it contains. If you take a look at the lives of most of these characters, you will see many seasons not characterized by faith. This chapter is not all about the glory of the people in it. It was not written for us to say, "Wow, they had it all together." It was penned for us to understand the source of their faith—the grace of God—and the fuel by which they were able to live through faith: the desire to be with God above all else.

This written tribute is filled with men and women who chose to draw near to God. The instances recorded in Hebrews 11 are events where they left behind every hindrance and sin. Comfort. Plans. Dreams. Power. Reputation. Doubt. All forsaken, to be with God. To remain in His presence. To stay in His will—His best plan for their life. And this pleased God.

These Hall of Faith members are witnesses to us that God is good. He is enough. He is all we need. They are heroes for us to study and listen to. As we intently lean into the Word over the next few weeks to hear what their lives echo through history, we will hear them saying, "God is enough. I don't need riches, security, or justice. I don't need my detailed plans or the approval of man. I don't need to achieve my goals, realize my dreams, or ascend to power. I only need to be with God."

As we march down the lengths of this Hall of Faith together and view the portraits hanging on the walls, I pray God would open our eyes to the

God-pleasing faith displayed by these men and women. In turn, may we also position our hearts toward drawing near.

> *I once thought these things were valuable, but now I consider them worthless because of what Christ has done. Yes, everything else is worthless when compared with the infinite value of knowing Christ Jesus my Lord. For his sake I have discarded everything else, counting it all as garbage, so that I could gain Christ and become one with him.*
>
> —Philippians 3:7–9 NLT

1. Open your time in the Word today with a prayer of thankfulness for God's merciful patience as we stumble through this daily faith walk. Ask Him to grant you a fresh joy to follow Him in obedient faith today. Journal your prayer below.

ENJOY EVERY WORD

We are going to accomplish two tasks together this week. We will study Hebrews 11:1–12, but we will also learn and establish a new way to study, using the FOCUSed15 study method.

2. Today, let's work through our first layer of studying Hebrews 11:1–12 by writing the passage. You can write the verse out word-for-word, diagram the sentences (like in fourth-grade English class), or even draw the passage with images that communicate each verse. Speak it, sing it, do whatever helps you slow down and enjoy what these verses communicate. There is no right or wrong way to do this. It is simply an exercise of intentionally taking in and enjoying each word. We'll build on what we learn from this practice through-out the rest of the week.

3. We're starting to see the main point of the passage. What do you think it might be? What do you think these verses communicate?

Abel offered. So did Cain. Each brother approached God with what looked like great gifts. Yet Cain is not among those counted as faithful. In fact (as we will see on Day 4), 1 John 3:12 tells us that he was "of the evil one" and his deeds were considered evil. Abel received commendation while

Cain received condemnation, and later proved the state of his wicked heart by murdering Abel out of jealousy. So what was the difference between Abel's "more acceptable sacrifice" and Cain's seemingly sacrificial gift? Their hearts. Abel gave through faith, out of a desire to be near the God he loved and served. We don't know the exact state of Cain's heart, but we can assume his primary concern was not intimacy with God. In fact, he may have lacked a relationship with God at all.

"The sacrifice of the wicked is an abomination to the LORD, but the prayer of the upright is acceptable to him" (Proverbs 15:8).

Let's learn from the example of Cain. Our actions are meaningless if we are not in right standing with God. You can attend church all your life and try to be the best person you can be, but it will all mean nothing (in fact, your self-righteous efforts will be an offense) without the grace of God covering your life. It is only by grace, through faith, that we can enter into fellowship with God. God's grace is extended to all—the greatest gift ever given—through the sacrifice of Christ. If you are uncertain of your position with God, I encourage you to read through the appendix on the gospel at the back of this study. Track down a friend or pastor who can explain anything you're not sure about. Don't rely on your actions to save you. The redeeming actions of Jesus alone can give us right standing with God.

Father God, You are holy, righteous, and yet incredibly merciful. Thank You for providing a way for me to experience an intimate relationship with You. Show me where I am clinging to self-righteousness instead of the righteousness provided by Christ. Be glorified in me as I live out my life with faith and draw near to Your presence in my every moment.

ⵢ BONUS STUDY ⵢ

Look up the outline for the Book of Hebrews in your study Bible or online resource. Read through the outline, and see where Hebrews 11 falls in the grand scheme of the Book of Hebrews.

Observation

FOCUSing ON HEBREWS 11:1–12

For by grace you have been saved through faith. And this is not your own doing; it is the gift of God, not a result of works, so that no one may boast.

—EPHESIANS 2:8–9

WE RECEIVE SALVATION through a saving faith in Jesus Christ. Through repentance of our sins and dependence on Christ's work on the Cross to pay the penalty for our sins, we can obtain eternal life. By God's grace, through our faith.

EPHESIANS 2:8–9

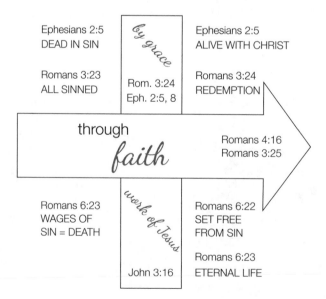

But have you ever wondered how people in Old Testament time received salvation? If they did not know about Jesus, as we know about Him today, how could they come to faith in someone who has not yet lived?

"And he [Abraham] believed the LORD, and he counted it to him as righteousness" (Genesis 15:6).

Before Christ came to earth, people came into a relationship with God the same way we do: by grace, through faith in God as the only provider of eternal life. Abraham did not receive right standing with God by his actions. His actions were proof of the state of his heart. Faith was the vehicle that brought righteousness into his life, and faith continued to be the way toward greater intimacy to his Savior.

God was not primarily pleased with the actions of early believers we will observe in our study today. Instead, it was their faith-filled heart that God commended.

1. Ask God to open your eyes and heart to receive encouragement from His Word. Declare your need for the Holy Spirit to illuminate and give insight. Thank Jesus for His work on the Cross, which gives eternal life and right standing before God.

LOOK AT THE DETAILS

2. Read Hebrews 11:1–12 and observe the truths about the actions our characters took. Ask yourself as you read, "What actions did this person take?"

It's very easy to inadvertently skip to interpretation (figuring out what this passage means), so be on guard for that. We're only gathering facts. Simply write what you see.

CHARACTERS	ACTIONS TAKEN
Abel (v. 4)	
Enoch (v. 5)	
Noah (v. 7)	
Abraham (v. 8–10, 12)	
Sarah (v. 11)	

The Bible tells us that Noah was "a righteous man, blameless in his generation" (Genesis 6:9), yet we later see him as a drunkard who lacked self-control and brought shame upon himself and his sons (Genesis 9:21–23). Sarah was blessed with a child because she considered God faithful, but only after she manipulated her husband to have a child with her maidservant—an attempt to subvert God's plan—and laughed when she received the news that she would bear a son. Abraham's long list of faith-filled deeds is impressive. However (out of fear of losing his own life and fortune), Abraham ordered his wife to tell others that they were siblings (not husband and wife), and allowed her to be taken away by another man. Twice.

If we view our Hebrews 11 heroes' actions (or our own) as the way to right standing with God, then we must also see their actions as a way they can lose God's eternal favor. Sinful choices certainly affect our intimacy with God and bring about earthly consequences, but if we have already made a declaration of saving faith—an unshakeable belief that the grace of God through the work of Christ alone can save us from our sin—we walk the journey ahead with confidence in our salvation from the power of sin. God has made a way for us to be with Him for eternity, and you and I stand on the other side of the mystery of Christ. Our Old Testament friends didn't know exactly how God was going to make a way, but they drew near in the confidence that He would do as He promised. Yet today we hold the living and active Word of God in our hands, which bears witness to the life, death, and Resurrection of Christ, and spells out clearly how we can enter into a relationship with God. By grace, through faith.

Bottom line: none of these individuals deserve to be commended. By us or by God. But God chose to show each of them mercy and favor. And it's from that provision of grace they were able to choose faith. And so it is with us.

"For who is God, but the LORD? And who is a rock, except our God?—the God who equipped me with strength and made my way blameless" (Psalm 18:31–32).

> God, I am thankful for the example of these faithful men and women. As I go about my day, help me to walk in faith as they did, drawing near to Your presence in the easy and the difficult. Holy Spirit, open my eyes to the everyday moments in which I can experience more of You through faith.

⚘ BONUS STUDY ⚘

Read Hebrews 11:1–12 and look for truths about faith and about God. Record your findings below. Write what the text shows, answering the questions "What is true about faith in this passage?" and "What is true about God in this passage?"

TRUTHS ABOUT FAITH	TRUTHS ABOUT GOD
Example: Assurance of things hoped for (v. 1)	*Example:* Created the universe by His word (v. 3)

CHEAT SHEET

2. Read Hebrews 11:1–12 and observe the truths about the actions our characters took. Ask yourself as you read, "What actions did this person take?"

CHARACTERS	ACTIONS TAKEN
Abel (v. 4)	Offered a more acceptable sacrifice to God than Cain
Enoch (v. 5)	Taken up to heaven by God, so that he did not see death
Noah (v. 7)	Responded to God's warning in reverent fear; constructed an ark for the salvation of his household
Abraham (vv. 8–10, 12)	Obeyed by faith; went to live in the unknown foreign land of promise; lived in tents with Isaac and Jacob; looked forward to the city that has foundations
Sarah (v. 11)	Received power to conceive; considered God faithful

BONUS STUDY CHEAT SHEET

TRUTHS ABOUT FAITH	TRUTHS ABOUT GOD
• Assurance of things hoped for (v. 1)	• Created the universe by His word (v. 3)
• Conviction of things not seen (v. 1)	• Commended Abel for his faith (v. 4)
• By it the "people of old" receive commendation (v. 2)	• Made Abel righteous by his faith (v. 4)
• By faith we observe things that are hard to understand (that the universe was created by God's word) (v. 3)	• Commended Abel by accepting his sacrifice (v. 4)
• Without faith it is impossible to please God (v. 6)	• God took Enoch to heaven before he died (v. 5)
• An inheritance of righteousness comes by faith (v. 7)	• Was pleased with Enoch (v. 5)
• Enabled Noah to act in reverent fear and obedience (v. 7)	• God is not pleased without faith (v. 6)
• Enabled Abraham to follow God's unclear leading in obedience (vv. 8–9)	• Warned Noah of events yet unseen (the flood) (v. 7)
• Enabled Sarah to believe in God's promise of a child (v. 11)	• Designer and builder of a city that has foundations (v. 10)
	• Considered by Sarah as faithful (v. 11)
	• Had promised Sarah a child (v. 11)

Clarification

FOCUSing ON HEBREWS 11:1–12

IN THE FIRST season of the ABC series *Once Upon a Time*, a young boy named Henry is on a quest to save his magical and mysterious home-town. The citizens of this town in Storybook, Maine, are in no way ordinary. Each of them is a character from a fairy tale and is now stuck in our world due to a curse. From Snow White and the Evil Queen to the crafts-man-father Geppetto and wooden-boy Pinocchio (and many more), the Storybook souls live a dissatisfying life void of the purpose and calling they were created to fulfill. On top of this, they've also been stripped of their magic and memories. As Henry grows up in Storybook and realizes he is not like everyone else, he sets out on a quest to find the "savior" (Emma), bring her to Storybook, and get her to deliver all the characters from their lost and aimless state.

Only there's a problem: Emma doesn't believe Henry's crazy story about the people who live there. The very one who holds the power to break the curse and restore the memories, magic, and mission of the characters doesn't want to have anything to do with them. If Henry wants to save Storybook, he must first get Emma to fully believe that the unseen realities of Storybook are true, and that she is the only one who can help them.

"And without faith it is impossible to please him, for whoever would draw near to God must believe that he exists and that he rewards those who seek him" (Hebrews 11:6).

If we desire to draw near to God, we must understand two things: He exists and He rewards. Seems pretty basic, but if we take a deep down look at our hearts, doubt often lingers around both of these truths. Maybe that's why we like the checklists and the hoops to jump through; they are easy, black-and-white ways to prove our faith in God. We may say we believe God exists, yet we make choices as if His existence bears no weight on our everyday. Sometimes the thoughts and beliefs of our mind need a deeper connection with the drive and desires of our heart.

It's easy to say I believe in God while surrounded by others who agree. But what if I find myself in hostile territory, where the very admission of faith in God would cost me my luxuries, my livelihood, or my life? A saving faith in God—who not only exists, but also is good, in control, and has a good purpose through every evil—will prevail in any environment.

"Faith is a settled confidence that something in the future—something that is not yet seen but has been promised by God—will actually come to pass because God will bring it about" (ESV Study Bible).

1. Take a few moments to look at your own heart. Is it connected with what you think and say you believe? Is your faith more than a comfortable faith, and will you believe that a loving God exists even when your surroundings are less than ideal?

UNCOVER THE ORIGINAL MEANING

My secondborn is well known in the Orr household as being the picky child. I get it. I'm known as being a picky eater, too. I like my coffee a certain way, and there are certain types of lettuce that just won't do. However, my sweet Anna is "sight" picky. If something doesn't look the way she thinks it should, she won't even try it. If I can somehow cajole her into trying whatever it is she has turned her nose to, most of the time she likes it!

Today is one of my favorite days of Bible study. I think it might become one of yours, too. We get to dive into the original language of the book of our passage: Greek. However, you might be a bit like Anna today, scared of what you see on your plate. I know new languages can seem a bit scary and maybe unpalatable, but I promise there are great rewards that await those who are willing to try it.

Studying Greek can be as easy as looking up a word in the dictionary. If this is your first attempt at Greek study, I encourage you to check out the videos I've created to show you how to use many of the online Greek tools. You can find them at KatieOrr.me/Resources. Let's walk through this process together.

Step 1: DECIDE which English word you would like to study.

To start your Greek study, look for any potential keywords in Hebrews 11:1–12. (If you are short on time, or this is your first time studying Greek, just pay attention to Hebrews 11:1.) As you find any repeated word or words that seem important to the passage, write them down below.

Maybe you have the word *faith* in your list? Let's study this word together.

Step 2: DISCOVER the Greek word in an interlinear Bible.

Now that we know what we want to study, we can look up the English word *faith* in an interlinear Bible to find out what the original Greek word is. An interlinear Bible will show you English verses and line up each word next to the Greek words they were translated from.

Let's take the first phrase in Hebrews 11:1 to see how this works:

"Now faith is the assurance of things hoped for . . ." (Hebrews 11:1).

In Greek, it looks like this: "ἔστιν δὲ πίστις ἐλπιζομένων."

Most people (including me!) can't read this, so the transliteration of the Greek is often provided for us as well. This transliteration is the Greek turned into words that use English letters to spell out how the Greek is read. For example, the first Greek words we see, ἔστιν and δὲ are transliterated into *estin* and *de,* which is how they are pronounced.

The interlinear Bible simply lines up the two versions (and usually the transliteration as well) so we can see which word goes with which, like this:

ἔστιν	δὲ	πίστις	ἐλπιζομένων
estin	de	pistis	elpizomenōn
is	now	faith	of things hoped for

Now you can use this layout to find the original word for *faith*. Do you see it? Faith=pistis=πίστις

Step 3: DEFINE that Greek word using a Greek lexicon.

Now that we know the original word for *faith* used in Hebrews 11:1 is *pistis*, we can look up that Greek word in a Greek lexicon (which is like a dictionary) and note the following:

Lexicon discovery: pistis
- Definition: faith, confidence, fidelity, guarantee, loyalty
- Times used: 243
- Part of speech: noun
- Other ways it is translated: assurance (once), belief (once)
- Any special notes: Strong's #4102 (I like to note the Strong's number, so later in my studies when I look up other words I can quickly see if it is the same word used or not.): "pistis, which derives from peithomai ('be persuaded, have confidence, obey'), connotes persuasion, conviction, and commitment, and always implies confidence, which is expressed in human relationships as fidelity, trust, assurance, oath, proof, guarantee. Only this richness of meaning can account for the faith (pistei, kata pistin, dia pisteōs) that inspired the conduct of the great Israelite ancestors of Hebrews 11."

Pretty simple, right?

2. Follow the previous steps for one other word. If this seems too overwhelming, consider choosing a word to look up in the dictionary, and then write out the definition. There is much to be learned even in that! Here are a few words to you could look up:

Pleased (v. 5)

Promised (v. 11)

Faithful (v. 11)

Lexicon discovery:

• Definition:

• Times used:

• Part of speech:

• Other ways it is translated:

• Any special notes:

3. What discoveries did you make through your clarification study? Which word did you learn the most about?

We may sometimes struggle to believe that God exists, but a more likely fight is the battle to believe that God "rewards those who seek him" (v. 6). Tucked away in verse 6, the Greek word *misthapodotēs*, which is defined as "one who pays wages:—rewarder" (Robert L. Thomas, *New American Standard Hebrew-Aramaic and Greek Dictionaries*). This rare Greek word is used only once in the New Testament: here in Hebrews 11:6, where we've been learning more about what faith is. It states that drawing near involves belief that God exists, but also that He is the misthapodotēs, the one who pays wages.

God is the one who gives us what we deserve.

Yet, the wages—what I earn because of my sin—is death. So if God owed any sort of payment to me, it's spiritual death and eternal separation from Him. However, (because of Jesus) this is no longer the case. Christ paid the debt of my sin—the death I earned—and exchanged it for His perfect righteousness and life eternal. What a great and glorious exchange!

Here we see, yet again, that faith is drawing near to our Holy God with a complete confidence that He will bring forth a payment of reward, not judgment. Dressed in the righteousness of Christ, I am able to seek the very presence of God, and as I make that choice to draw near, my misthapodotēs God showers me with the rewards of His grace.

"For the wages of sin is death, but the free gift of God is eternal life in Christ Jesus our Lord" (Romans 6:23).

> *God, I don't deserve Your great kindness. I am so thankful for the ability to draw near and no longer fear condemnation or the wage I deserve. Thank You, Jesus, for paying the debt my sin incurred, and for lavishly pouring out Your grace on me. Help me to continually draw near in faith that You will reward, not condemn.*

⁖ BONUS STUDY ⁖

Look up additional words throughout each verse in this week's passage.

CHEAT SHEET

Step 3: DEFINE that Greek word using a Greek lexicon.

Pleased (v. 5): euarestev

• Definition: cause to be pleased

• Times used: 3

• Type of word: verb

• Other ways it is translated: none

• Any special notes: Strong's #2100: all three uses in Hebrews (11:5, 6; 13:16).

Promised (v. 11): epangellomai

• Definition: to promise; assert

• Times used: 15

• Type of word: verb

• Other ways it is translated: to promise, profess, make promise

• Any special notes: Strong's #1861

Faithful (v. 11): pistos

• Definition: faithful

• Times used: 67

• Type of word: adjective

• Other ways it is translated: faith/faithful, believe, trustworthy, sure

• Any special notes: Strong's #4103

Utilization

FOCUSing ON HEBREWS 11:1–12

Blessed Lord, let me climb up near to thee, and love, and long, and plead, and wrestle with thee, and pant for deliverance from the body of sin, for my heart is wandering and lifeless, and my soul mourns to think it should ever lose sight of its Beloved. Wrap my life in divine love, and keep me ever desiring thee, always humble and resigned to thy will, more fixed on thyself, that I may be more fitted for doing and suffering.

—"Longings After God," *The Valley of Vision: a Collection of Puritan Prayers and Devotions*

EVERYDAY FAITH IS not about trying harder. Living a life marked by the presence of Christ is about believing better. Instead of trying to make God love and accept me, I must stand on the promise that I am already forgiven, accepted, and righteous in God's sight. When He looks at me, He is pleased! Nothing I can do today will make Him love me more. Nothing I do tomorrow will cause Him to love me less. When I truly and deeply understand this reality, it changes everything. My affections for the thrills of this world diminish and my desire increases for my every moment to be in the presence of God. The longing for approval and accolades that puts me in overdrive to prove my sufficiency is taken over with a desire to linger in the love of Christ, reminding me that I don't need to be enough. Jesus is enough on my behalf.

So, when my everyday feels faithless, I must take a step back and remember who I really am. Approved. Loved. Set apart for God's glory. And when I take the time to remember who I am because of Jesus, my affections are stirred for more of His presence. I draw near because I desire to live in the righteous, royal path my loving King has chosen for me, rather than the dirty ditch I often fall into. This is what I need to remember: God's presence is what my spirit truly wants. The love of Jesus is what my heart really needs. The stirring of the Holy Spirit is the excitement my soul craves. Walking with God takes work, but it must be fueled by a simple desire to be near God, instead of a desire to prove ourselves to God.

1. Think back on the last month or so of your life. Circle below which of the two best describes your spiritual efforts of late.

Trying Harder   Believing Better

Spend a few moments in remembrance of all God has done for you. Thank Him for His mercy and grace. Ask the Holy Spirit to help you believe better as you continue to follow God in your day-to-day.

DISCOVER THE CONNECTIONS

2. Look up the following Old Testament references to add to what you've already learned about each character's actions (take a peek back at your chart on Day 2 if you need a refresher), and then head back to Hebrews 11 to look for details about how each character received right standing before God. Record any additional details you learn about Abel, Enoch, and Noah in the chart below. (We will focus more on Sarah and Abraham next week.)

CHARACTER	ACTIONS TAKEN (BY FAITH, THEY DID WHAT?)	MENTIONS OF PLEASING GOD/RECEIVING RIGHTEOUSNESS
Abel: Genesis 4:4 (Read all of Genesis 4:1–5 if you have additional time.)		
Enoch: Genesis 5:24 (Read all of Genesis 5:21–24 if you have additional time.)		
Noah: Genesis 6:9 (Read all of Genesis 6:5–22 if you have additional time.)		

We know very little of Enoch's story, but we do know this: he walked with God, was commended as having pleased God, and was taken by God up to heaven to be with Him. God's purpose for Enoch on this earth was done so He brought this faithful man home. In my pursuits to be near God, I often forget His desire to be near me. As much as I long to be in fellowship with Him, He wants it more. It's His will for me to dwell in His presence and everything He allows me to experience on this earth—the good and the bad—is to point me to Him. He reveals more and more of Himself to me every day, and as I learn to be still and know that He is God (Psalm 46:10), I see Him in the seemingly meaningless and mundane, as well as in His beautiful and bountiful provisions. As I draw near through faith in every circumstance, I will experience the nearness of God more and more.

"Draw near to God, and he will draw near to you" (James 4:8).

*Father, help me to see You in my everyday moments.
I want to know You more intimately, hear You more clearly,
and see You more fully.*

⸪ BONUS STUDY ⸪

Look up the following cross-references from this week's passage. If you have additional time, follow all the cross-references in your study Bible or free online resource. You could easily spend two or three days, 15 minutes or more at a time, working through each verse. Remember, these days are simply suggestions. Follow God's leading. If He tells you to slow down and dig deep, go for it!

Hebrews 11:1 — "things not seen"
2 Corinthians 4:17–18
2 Corinthians 5:7
1 Peter 1:8

11:7 — "the righteousness that comes by faith"
Romans 4:13

11:12 — "him as good as dead"
Romans 4:19–22

CHEAT SHEET

2. Look up the following Old Testament references to add to what you've already learned about each character's actions (take a peek back at your chart on Day 2 if you need a refresher), and then head back to Hebrews 11 to look for details about how each character received right standing before God. Record any additional details you learn about Abel, Enoch, and Noah in the chart below. (We will focus more on Sarah and Abraham next week.)

CHARACTER	ACTIONS TAKEN (BY FAITH, THEY DID WHAT?)	MENTIONS OF PLEASING GOD/RECEIVING RIGHTEOUSNESS
Abel Genesis 4:4 Hebrews 11:4	Brought a sacrifice of the firstborn of his flock	Commended as righteous through his sacrifice God commended him by accepting his gifts
Enoch Genesis 5:24 Hebrews 11:5	Walked with God	Commended as having pleased God (before he was taken up)
Noah Genesis 6:9 Hebrews 11:7	Walked with God	Became an heir of righteousness that comes by faith; righteous man, blameless

BONUS STUDY CHEAT SHEET

11:1 "things not seen"

2 Corinthians 4:17–18

>Things that are seen are temporary

>Things that are unseen are eternal

>The unseen is an eternal weight of glory, beyond all comparison

>We are to look to the unseen

2 Corinthians 5:6–7

>While we are here on this earth, we are away from the presence of God

>We walk by faith, not by sight.

1 Peter 1:8

>Though we have not seen God we:

>• Love Him

>• Believe in Him

>• Rejoice with inexpressible joy

>• Rejoice with joy filled with glory

11:7—"the righteousness that comes by faith"

Romans 4:13

>The promise that came to Abraham came through the righteousness that comes by faith.

>Abraham did not become the father of many nations because he was righteous. The promises he received were not a direct result of his works or by following the Old Testament Law. He received promises by God's grace, which were realized through Abraham's faith.

11:12—"him as good as dead"

Romans 4:19–22

(I love this passage! There are many truths about Abraham here to notice.)

Abraham did not weaken in faith, even when everything pointed to the absolute physical impossibility of having a son.

- His body was "good as dead."
- He was about 100 years old.
- Sarah was barren (she could not have any children.)
- Held an unwavering belief in God's promises to him.
- Grew strong in his faith.
- Gave glory to God while he was still waiting for the promise!
- He was fully convinced that God was *able* to do what He promised. His faith was counted to him as righteousness.

Summation

FOCUSing ON HEBREWS 11:1–12

Let us read our Bibles reverently and diligently, with an honest determination to believe and practice all we find in them. It is no light matter how we use this book. Eternal life or death depends on the spirit in which it is used.

—J. C. RYLE

I LOVE A good checklist. I start off most of my days with a 3x5 card filled with handwritten to-dos, and I love being able to throw away that paper full of little boxes and scribbles at the end of the day. Completed. Accomplished. Achieved.

Check.

Today we will attempt to summarize all we've learned so far and apply it. Unfortunately, attempts at application can often look a lot like my daily checklists. Do better. Try harder. Pray more. Memorize a Bible verse. Go to church.

Check. Check. Check.

But that's not what we've learned this week about living the life of faith, is it? Pursuing God is not an accomplishment to achieve. I will not be graded at the end of the day on my performance. Living a faith-filled day is about stirring my affections for God, not amplifying my good actions.

The crazy thing is, the more we long for God, the more our actions and attitudes look more like Him, and the very item on our list we most seek to check off becomes a closer reality.

1. Spend a few moments, in preparing your heart for today's time with God. Confess any tendencies to make application a checklist, instead of a pursuit of His presence. Ask God to show you what it looks like to apply His Word through a deeper faith in His goodness.

RESPOND TO GOD'S WORD

IDENTIFY: What's the main idea?

2. Write out the main idea of Hebrews 11:1–12.

3. Read a commentary or study Bible to see how your observations line up. As you search the commentaries, ask God to make clear the meaning of any passages that are fuzzy to you. Record any additional observations.

If you still have any lingering questions about this week's verse, ask a trusted pastor, mentor, or friend what they think about the verse, or enter the online discussion at BibleStudyHub.com.

MODIFY: How do my beliefs line up to this main idea?

Journal through the following questions:

4. How does your view of faith line up with what you've learned this week? Do you believe true faith is more about your affections for God than your actions for God? Do you try to prove your faith primarily through actions, or do you see the fruit of faith in your life as a result of a deeper relationship with God?

5. How does your view of God line up with what you've learned this week?

GLORIFY: In light of this main idea, how can I realign my life to best reflect God's glory?

We exist to bring glory to God. Like the moon that reflects the glory of the sun, we are satellites to show off God's blazing glory to those around us. Application is not digging down deep within ourselves so we can try harder and do better. Application is an alignment; a coming back to the One who is at work within us and allowing Him to do as He wills, so that we can show Him glorious to those around us. Studying God's Word helps us see the adjustments needed to better depend on God and reflect His glory.

6. How could believing the truths discovered in Hebrews 11:1–12 affect your everyday moments?

7. What adjustments can you make to glorify God in your atti-

tudes and actions this week?

Abel offered. Enoch was taken up. Noah constructed. Abraham went.
Sarah received. Each of our heroes displayed faith in very different ways.
Yet we're told they all "received their commendation" (Hebrews 11:2).
God was pleased with each of them. Yet, it wasn't the actions themselves
that God was pleased with, it was the position of their hearts while act-
ing. Because God is not as concerned with our actions as He is our heart.
You and I could lead the same "Christian" life, and make all the "right"
decisions, but it doesn't guarantee we are living a life of faith.

Today's churches are filled with men and women living faithless lives.
They make it to church when they can, sing the songs, listen to the sermon, shake some hands, maybe even drop something in the offering, but
they are not any closer to God than the soul who has yet to step in the
halls of a church building.

Faith is not primarily about our actions. Faith is about our affections.
When my heart is set on being with God, my life will be filled with the
evidence of His presence; the natural result of inviting God into every
part of my life is a life filled with contagious faith.

> God, I am so thankful for Your Word! I know that every pas-
> sage, verse, and word is there with great purpose and for my
> good. As I study the lives of these men and women of faith,
> open my heart to learn from their successes and failures.
> Thank You for providing these heroes to look to. Today, help
> me to pursue Your presence more than anything.

⊰ BONUS STUDY ⊱

Chose a few verses from our passage to memorize. Write them out on a 3x5 card, and post them up around your house in prominent places to help you remember the truths you've learned this week.

FOCUSING ON **HEBREWS 11:13–28**

Perspective in Drawing Near

Foundation

FOCUSing ON HEBREWS 11:13–28

EARLY ON A dark Atlanta morning, alongside a team of local college students and a few other Campus Crusade campus ministry staff, my husband Chris and I excitedly boarded a plane to begin our long 24-hour trip to Asia. With a backpack and two bags each, we headed down the jet bridge toting our seven-month-old son in a grey umbrella stroller. Chris, Baby Kenneth, and I spent a summer in a large university town filled with an unthinkable amount of smog—ubiquitous soot that settled into every surface—and a huge population of unbelieving students who had yet to hear the good news about Jesus. For six weeks, we lived on campus with a prayerful purpose to find the students God had for us to bring the gospel to.

Our little family stayed in a small campus apartment, dusted with the aforementioned soot, and filled with fire code violations and electrical hazards not seen in American buildings for decades. I bathed my baby in pathogen-laden waters. We slept on a stiff, flat mattress that seemed as hard as plywood. Every spiritual conversation we had indoors or on a phone was spoken in code, as our rooms, phone calls, and emails were most undoubtedly bugged.

Though we were surrounded by many discomforts and dangers not experienced in our American home, we knew our time overseas was short and very significant. It took a few days to get used to, but the remaining time was spent with great purpose, fulfilling the mission for which we were sent. Throughout our time, one fact remained. We were aliens. We did not belong there, and we stuck out every place we travelled.

It's been almost a decade since we took that trip across the globe, yet I often forget that I am still a foreigner. America is where I reside, but I am a sojourner. I am not really home. (Neither are you.) In many ways, I ought to feel the same today as I did in that uncomfortable, dirty, tiny Asian apartment—unsettled, longing for more, but knowing that there are good things to come. My time on earth is short and needs to be filled with purpose and great intentionality. Knowing that we had only weeks in that space, it would have been ridiculous for Chris and me to spend all our time, life savings, and efforts toward making our Asian summer apartment more comfortable. Yet, I all too often waste precious resources making this temporary life more comfortable; I've been given means (time, energy, money, gifting, etc.) that are meant for God's eternal purposes, not my immediate satisfaction.

"We are here for only a moment, visitors and strangers in the land as our ancestors were before us. Our days on earth are like a passing shadow, gone so soon without a trace" (1 Chronicles 29:15 NLT).

Living a life of faith includes making choices in light of eternity. We will see this in our studies this week. Men and women who are filled with faith view themselves as foreigners; they are sojourners on their way to a deeper place with God. True followers of Christ are to walk in obedience along a foundation of faith that there is more to this life than what we see, and they view themselves as aliens looking forward to a day when that faith will be made sight.

1. Journal out a prayer of dependence on the Holy Spirit's work in your heart

and mind to understand the depths of what we will read and study this week. Thank Him ahead of time for all that He will reveal.

ENJOY EVERY WORD

2. Read through Hebrews 11:13–28 and then rewrite the passage. Remember, there are lots of different ways you can do this foundation work (a simple rewrite, diagram sentences, read it aloud, draw out what you see, etc.). Do whatever helps you slow down and take in each word.

This journey toward our true homeland is a battle of faith—a confidence in God's good character and a hope in all there is to come. The Hall of Faith is filled with such forward-looking faith. I pray that as we move on to our studies for the week, God will show us where we are clinging more to our temporary home than we are drawing near to His presence.

> *God, I confess I am much too comfortable here on earth. I spend my time and resources on my selfish pleasures, more than I do on Your eternal purposes. Holy Spirit, open my eyes to the everyday opportunities I have to display faith as I draw near to Your presence here on earth. Use me for Your glory!*

.¡. BONUS STUDY .¡.

Read through all of Hebrews 11 and give your best attempts at an outline for the chapter. There is no right or wrong, just section it out as you see natural breaks. After you try your hand at it, you can see my attempts in the cheat sheet.

BONUS STUDY CHEAT SHEET

There are many approaches to outlining this chapter. Here is mine:

Faith defined (vv. 1–3)

    1: Faith is assurance of things hoped for, conviction of things not seen

    2: Commendation is received through faith displayed

    3: Understanding of the invisible comes through faith

Preflood: From Abel to Noah (vv. 4–5)

    4: By faith Abel

    5: By faith Enoch

Faith defined (v. 6–7)

    6: Without faith it is impossible to please God.

    7: Drawing near to God takes faith in His good, rewarding character

Patriarchs of Israel: From Abraham and Sarah (vv. 8–12)

    8–10: By faith Abraham

    11: By faith Sarah

    12: Therefore, descendants were born

    13–16: These all died in faith, as sojourners

Patriarchs of Israel: From Abraham to Joseph (vv. 17–22)

    17–19: By faith Abraham

    20: By faith Isaac

    21: By faith Jacob

    22: By faith Joseph

The Exodus (vv. 23–29)

> 23: By faith Moses's parents
>
> 24–28: By faith Moses
>
> 29: By faith Israelites crossed Red Sea

Israelite Conquest and Judges (vv. 30–35a)

> 30: By faith Israelites defeated Jericho
>
> 31: By faith Rahab
>
> 32–35a: By faith many more experienced victory

Unnamed Heroes With Undesirable Outcomes (vv. 35b–38)

These all commended through their faith, but still waiting for perfection (vv. 39–40)

Observation

FOCUSing ON HEBREWS 11:13–28

IF YOU GREW up in church (and maybe even if you didn't) you know that Father Abraham had many sons, and many sons had Father Abraham. (And now you will have that sweet song in your head for the rest of the day. Enjoy.) I grew up in Christian school and learned a lot about Abraham and many other characters in our Hall of Faith. However, I never understood why the actions of these men and women were important, or how to apply the details of those actions to my own life.

Abraham almost sacrificed his son Isaac, but God intervened at the last minute with a ram to use instead. Moses was put in a basket as a baby then grew up to emancipate the Israelite slaves in Egypt through the plagues and parting of the Red Sea. Though I never voiced my thoughts, I often wondered, "So what? How does this apply to me?"

The older I grew the more often I came to ask these questions and more. At first glance, the lives told of in the Bible seem so far removed from anything I have or will experience. How could I relate these lessons to my life? What do a colorful coat, the plagues of Egypt, and a ram caught in a bush have to do with me? Yet, as we see these stories in light of the full counsel of Scripture, we come to know there is more to view about these stories than what meets the eye, and there is much we can learn about the heart of faith-filled living from those who went before us.

1. As you begin, ask God to open your eyes to the thread of faith that runs through each life represented in these verses.

LOOK AT THE DETAILS

2. Read Hebrews 11:13–16 and observe the truths about the actions our characters took. Ask yourself, as you read, "What actions did this person take?" It's very easy to inadvertently skip to interpretation (figuring out what this passage means), so be on guard for that. We're only gathering facts. Simply write what you see.

CHARACTERS	ACTIONS TAKEN
Abraham (v. 17–19)	
Isaac (v. 20)	
Jacob (v. 21)	
Joseph (v. 22)	
Moses's parents (v. 23)	
Moses (v. 24–28)	

3. Which of these truths stands out to you? What evidence do you see of an eternal perspective in their choices?

Temptations abound daily, and the key to overcoming them boils down to what I treasure most. (And a whole lot of God's enabling grace to choose well.) Abraham chose the fellowship of God over his precious son and promised legacy. In blessing their own sons, Isaac and Jacob, both chose to cling to the hope of God's covenant relationship with them, instead of giving in to anxiety and fear of what might be around the corner. By giving burial directions, Joseph displayed a confidence in God's faithful provision and future deliverance for the people of Israel. Moses chose God over royal status, physical comfort, and worldly pleasure.

Every allurement I face is an opportunity to show God as my greatest treasure—what I truly want. Every choice to sin is a decision to cherish something else over Jesus.

> God, create in me a greater desire for You! Strip away the passions and pursuits of this world. I want to want You more. Open my eyes to see the appetites of my heart that get in the way of my devotion to You.

⨯ BONUS STUDY ⨯

Read Hebrews 11:13–16, looking for what is true about "these all" and their eternal perspective.

EXAMPLE: died in faith (v. 13)

CHEAT SHEET

2. Read Hebrews 11:13–16 and observe the truths about the actions our characters took. Ask yourself, as you read, "What actions did this person take?" It's very easy to inadvertently skip to interpretation (figuring out what this passage means), so be on guard for that. We're only gathering facts. Simply write what you see.

CHARACTER	ACTION TAKEN
Abraham	• Offered up Isaac (v. 17) • Believed that God was able to raise Isaac from the dead, if he had to die (v. 19)
Isaac	• Invoked future blessings on his sons, Jacob and Esau (v. 20)
Jacob	• Blessed each of the sons of Joseph (his grandsons) on his deathbed (v. 21) • Bowing in worship over the head of his staff (v. 21)
Joseph	• At the end of his life made mention of the exodus of the Israelites (v. 22) • Gave directions concerning his bones (v. 22)
Moses's Parents	• Hid Moses for three months (v. 23) • Did not fear the king's edict (v. 23)
Moses	• Refused to be called the son of Pharaoh's daughter (v. 24) • Chose to be mistreated with the people of God when he could have enjoyed the fleeting pleasures of sin (v. 25) • His desire to please Christ was greater than the desire for wealth (v. 26) • Had an eternal perspective; looked to the reward (v. 26) Left Egypt (v. 27) • Did not fear the king more than he feared God (v. 27) Endured (v. 27) • Saw Him who is invisible (v. 27) • Kept the first Passover and sprinkled the blood on his doorposts (v. 28)

BONUS STUDY CHEAT SHEET

Read Hebrews 11:13–16, looking for what is true about "these all" and their eternal perspective:

Died in faith (v. 13)

Did not receive the things promised (v. 13)

Saw the things promised from afar (v. 13)

Acknowledged they were strangers and exiles on the earth (v. 13)

Sought a homeland (v. 14)

Desired a better country, a heavenly one (v. 16)

God is not ashamed of them (v. 16)

Have a city prepared for them by God (v. 16)

Clarification

FOCUSing ON HEBREWS 11:13–28

GOD'S GRACE CHANGES us. We are given a new nature, a new identity, and a new lens from which we view our days. The more we understand the depths of God's love for us, and the sacrifice Jesus made for us, the more we see life through the eyes of faith. And the more we wear the glasses of everyday faith, the more an eternal perspective colors each of our moments.

Washing dishes, creating spreadsheets, chatting with a neighbor, or tucking little ones into bed can all be carried out with eternity in mind. We are strangers here, remember? Each and every day is part of the journey home. Every breath we take is willed by God and meant for His glory. You read these words today because God has allowed you another day on this earth, for a purpose.

How we view ourselves is a big deal. If we don't see ourselves as sojourners, we won't live like sojourners.

1. Spend a few moments acknowledging to God the places where you have a hard time believing "that task" can be a part of His plan. Ask Him for a change in perspective, to see every day, every moment, as a step closer to His presence and our ultimate home.

UNCOVER THE ORIGINAL MEANING

Step 1: DECIDE which English word you would like to study.

To start your Greek study, look for any potential key words in Hebrews 11:13–28. As you find any repeated words or words that seem important to the passage, write them down below. If you are short on time today, focus on verses 13–16. (Note to beginners: If you are overwhelmed with the newness of another language, simply pick out two or three words to look up in a dictionary, and note anything that opens up the meaning of the passage to you.)

Step 2: DISCOVER the Greek word in an interlinear Bible.

There are so many great words to look up, but I want to make sure you look up at least one today: *acknowledged* (your version might say *agreed, confessed,* or *admitted*). Using an interlinear Bible, find the original word for *acknowledged* used in the last sentence of verse 13 and write it below.

Step 3: DEFINE that Greek word using a Greek lexicon.

Now we can look up the Greek word in a Greek lexicon (which is like a dictionary) and note the following:

Lexicon discovery: acknowledged (v. 13)

• Definition:

• Times used:

• Part of speech:

• Other ways it is translated:

• Any special notes:

2. Follow the steps above to look up one more word. You can choose one of your words from Step 1, or choose one from the list below:

Greeted (v. 13)

Called (v. 16)

Lexicon discovery:
- Definition:
- Times used:
- Part of speech:
- Other ways it is translated:
- Any special notes:

3. What discoveries did you make through your clarification study? Which word did you learn the most about?

These sojourners made choices out of faith. Faith that there is something better, something greater than what they held dear on this earth. They let go of dreams, power, and pleasure to take hold of the treasures of Christ, and looked to all that God promised. In so doing they homologeō (11:13)—they confessed allegiance—that their faith is in the God of heaven alone. Not in man. Not in themselves. Not in their hopes and dreams. They trusted in God alone. We, too, must *homologeō;* admit that this world is not our home and take hold of all God has planned for us as foreigners in this land.

God, give me the grace to let go of my dreams, comforts, and fears so that I may place my faith solely in You. You are God alone. You are worthy of my trust. I long to be near You more than anything. Today, give me a greater desire for my true home that will grow with every day you give me on this earth.

⋅⋅ BONUS STUDY ⋅⋅

Look up additional words throughout each verse in this week's passage.

CHEAT SHEET

Step 3: DEFINE that Greek word using a Greek lexicon.

Acknowledged (v. 13): homologeō

• Definition: confess, admit

• Times used: 26

• Part of speech: verb

• Other ways it is translated: confess, promised, declare, granted, made, profess

• Any special notes: Strong's #3670: "profess, to confess allegiance"

Greeted (v. 13): aspazomai

• Definition: greet; be happy about; welcome

• Times used: 59

• Part of speech: verb

• Other ways it is translated: greet, salute, farewell, embrace

• Any special notes: Strong's #782

Called (v. 16): epikaleō

• Definition: invoke; appeal

• Times used: 30

• Part of speech: verb

• Other ways it is translated: appeal, name

• Any special notes: Strong's #1941: "be people of, formally, those who call upon the name; this means that they are one of God's people"

Utilization

FOCUSING ON HEBREWS 11:13–28

THE STORY OF Moses is a familiar one for most. As a baby he was delivered from a slaughtering edict that threatened to remove every Hebrew baby from Egypt. Discovered by the Pharaoh's daughter, Moses was adopted into the royal family and raised as an Egyptian. As an adult, with every pleasure and resource available at his command, he chose to leave it all behind to follow God. After discovering an undeniable call of God on his life, he forsook the familiar, luxurious, and secure for the disruptive, difficult, and uncertain. Moses knew the source of his true satisfaction and joy—the treasure of life with God—and repeatedly resolved to draw near to the God who faithfully led his steps. A true sojourner, Moses spent the rest of his days one foot in front of the other, following the guiding presence of God to the Promised Land.

Moses certainly had his moments of self-doubt and failure, but his lifetime is still an example of faith you and I can learn from. Though our circumstances are much different, our human desires for security and comfort are the same. Again and again, Moses chose obedient faith over selfish apathy, and drew near to the presence of God.

1. Think back on the last week. How have you spent your time, money, and resources? Have your choices brought you closer or further from God?

2. Ask God to increase your desire for His presence. Thank Him for His faithfulness as your Lord and Savior.

DISCOVER THE CONNECTIONS

Today we'll take a deeper look at Moses and his everyday choices of faith.

3. Look up each cross-reference below about Moses and take notes from any verses that bring clarity to this passage. If you have additional time, use your study Bible or online tool to look up additional cross-references.

VERSE FROM HEBREWS	PHRASE TO STUDY	CROSS-REFERENCE	NOTES
11:25	"choosing rather"	Pslam 84:10	
11:25	"the fleeting pleasures of sin"	1 John 2:17	
11:26	"He considered the reproach of Christ great wealth"	Philippians 3:7–11	

In Philippians 3, we see a beautiful picture of craving the presence of Christ above all else. Stirring our affections for Christ is sure to give us a greater longing for heaven. Because it is there in heaven that Jesus is seated at the right hand of God, waiting to embrace and reward those who seek Him with His eternal presence.

If I'm honest, I don't always desire heaven. Yes, I know that it's my true homeland, but it seems so far away and hard to imagine. I forget that it isn't just about the place of heaven that my soul longs for, it's being in the presence of God and receiving the promises of His Word; both of which will be fully revealed and experienced in heaven. My heavenly homeland is where my salvation is realized in every way. Scholars call heaven the consummation of salvation.

It's important to understand that there are three parts to our salvation. When we first come to saving faith in Christ, we are granted right standing with God—justification. Positionally, we are given a new nature and a great inheritance as part of God's family. Though we are delivered from the penalty of our sin, as long as we are on this earth, we will wrestle with the presence of sin in our lives. Once justified, until the day we meet Jesus face-to-face, believers live in the second part of our salvation—sanctification. Day-by-day, and by His Spirit, we become more and more like Jesus as we walk in faith of all God has done and will continue to do in us. And then, one glorious day, either by death or the return of Christ, we will reach the culmination of our salvation—consummation. Until then, we walk this earth as sojourners to our final destination, where all we've begun to know and experience through Christ will become perfectly complete as we enter into the full, unhindered presence of our glorious God. (Check out my *Everyday Hope* FOCUSed15 Bible study for a deeper study on the three parts to our salvation.)

In our curiosity about all heaven might and will be, we often lose sight of the most important part of heaven: the consummation of all we look forward to. We do not sojourn on this temporary earth primarily to enjoy our heavenly mansions and streets of gold. We are journeying toward the full and transforming presence of Christ. Heaven itself is not the reward. Being with Christ is the reward.

"But our citizenship is in heaven, and from it we await a Savior, the Lord Jesus Christ" (Philippians 3:20).

> *God, give me a longing for heaven as the saints of old had. Loosen the grip that the things of this earth have on my heart. Strip away the distractions and competitions that settle me into a place that is not my ultimate home. Help me to see how I can free up my time, money, and talents to be used for Your glory.*

⁂ BONUS STUDY ⁂

Choose additional words and phrases and follow the cross-references in your study Bible or free online resource.

CHEAT SHEET

3. Look up each cross-reference below about Moses and take notes from any verses that bring clarity to this passage. If you have additional time, use your study Bible or online tool to look up additional cross-references.

VERSE FROM HEBREWS	PHRASE TO STUDY	CROSS-REFERENCE	NOTES
11:25	"choosing rather"	Psalm 84:10	• A day in the presence of God is better than a thousand elsewhere. • God's presence is our greatest treasure!
11:25	"the fleeting pleasures of sin"	1 John 2:17	• This world is passing away.
11:26	"He considered the reproach of Christ great wealth"	Philippians 3:7–11	• Whatever I gain, it is nothing compared to the surpassing worth of Christ. • Knowing Christ is the highest worth. • We are to count all things as rubbish, in order to gain Christ and be found in Him. • We have no righteousness on our own. • We have a righteousness that comes through faith in Christ. • We count all as loss so that we might know Christ and His power. • We share in His sufferings and Resurrection.

Summation

FOCUSing ON HEBREWS 11:13–28

IN THIS WEEK'S passage we begin to see another component of the thread of faith that runs throughout the Old and New Testament. In Hebrews 11:13 (and later in v. 39), the author adds that though these men and women died in faith, they didn't received what was promised.

Wait a minute. Last week we looked at Sarah, who by faith conceived and later gave birth to Isaac. The same Isaac we studied this week in verse 20. What was promised—a son of Abraham—was fulfilled through the birth of Isaac. So, why would the author say that she and the others died in faith without receiving what was promised? The promise to Sarah must be for more than just a baby boy.

"But as it is, they desire a better country, that is, a heavenly one" (Hebrews 11:16).

They were each promised a better, permanent home. A heavenly homeland. A city filled with the forever presence of God. And it was by faith in this future fulfillment that they each chose what they did. They left behind comfort, pleasures, and what they held most dear on this earth to sojourn toward eternal fellowship with God.

Living as an alien is uncomfortable. No one likes to be the stranger in the room. We each have a God-given craving to belong, but we must consider the reality that nothing and no one on this earth will satisfy that hunger.

"Beloved, I urge you as sojourners and exiles to abstain from the passions of the flesh, which wage war against your soul" (1 Peter 2:11).

The passions of the flesh Peter mentions here may not always be the big no-nos. Deliberate sins are certainly going to hinder our faith-walk with Christ. However (as we looked at in Week 1), even the seemingly harmless can hinder us from running this race well. You and I do not belong here on this earth. We are foreigners sojourning on this road toward heaven, and as much as our desire for security and comfort beckons us to put down roots into the soil of this earth, we are called to live uprooted; ready to pick up and go at a moment's notice, with our time, money, and talents at His disposal.

Each of our characters demonstrates their desire for the nearness of God through their faith in the unlikely, impossible, and uncomfortable. Their choices of obedience showed God as supreme in their life. Their desire to please God more than man was shown through their decisions of faith.

1. As we move toward applying all we've learned this week, begin with a time of soul searching. Ask the Holy Spirit to reveal in you the places where you are acting out of something other than a desire for God. Confess those places to Him and ask Him for a growing desire to be with Him. Thank Him for His grace.

RESPOND TO GOD'S WORD

IDENTIFY: What's the main idea?

2. Write out the main idea of Hebrews 11:13–28.

3. Read a commentary or study Bible to see how your observations line up. As you search the commentaries, ask God to make clear the meaning of any passages that are fuzzy to you. Record any additional observations.

If you still have any lingering questions about this week's verse, ask a trusted pastor, mentor, or friend what they think about the verse, or enter the online discussion at BibleStudyHub.com.

MODIFY: How do my beliefs line up to this main idea?

Journal through the following questions:

4. How does your view of faith line up with what you've learned this week?

5. What are you treasuring more than the presence of Christ?

GLORIFY: In light of this main idea, how can I realign my life to best reflect God's glory?

6. How could believing the truths discovered in Hebrews 11:13–28 affect your everyday moments?

7. What adjustments can you make to glorify God in your attitudes and actions this week?

God, I am so thankful for Your grace. Continue to open my eyes to see the passions, people, and pursuits that I have put before You. You are greater. You are worth all of my affections. Change my heart. Holy Spirit, fill every space of my life. Bring forth a great change in me, for Your glory.

⚜ BONUS STUDY ⚜

Chose a few verses from our passage to memorize. Write them out on a 3x5 card and post them up around your house in prominent places to help you remember the truths we've learned this week.

FOCUSING ON **HEBREWS 11:29–40**

Perfection in Drawing Near

Foundation

FOCUSing ON HEBREWS 11:29–40

MY HUSBAND'S GRANDMOTHER Leona is a nurturing, caring woman. MeMaw tirelessly works, even at her old age, to keep her home in order, cook, and bake yummy treats for others. A true servant. She is also a pretty funny lady, though she doesn't always mean to be. You see, MeMaw is losing her hearing, which leads to some funny moments.

One sunny day, we all stood chatting in her kitchen, looking out the window to her backyard. Several weeks before, she had a dying tree removed from the center of the grassy area. My mother-in-law, Rhonda, excitedly mentioned to MeMaw that she had grass growing up to cover the dirt patch that remained where the tree once stood. This is where the story turns funny.

"Mother," Rhonda exclaims, "you have grass!"

MeMaw's face contorted in disgust and exclaimed, "Rats?!"

And everyone lost it, in laughter. That one word, in just the right tone, was so out of place in the conversation no one in the room could help but laugh.

There is a similar shift in this week's passage, though missing the light-hearted humor. It's easy to see why Rahab, David, Samson, and the like are listed in the Hall of Faith. Their obedient choices give us example after example of faith-filled living to look to. Yet, there is a dramatic shift in verse 35; a seemingly random account that doesn't look to fit the occasion.

After a long list of men and women who saw God's miraculous deliverance and enabling power, another list emerges. The tortured, the suffering, the destitute. Author of Hebrews . . . did I hear you right? Torture? Prison? Death? This is faith? Is this correct, or am I in need of a hearing aid?

We will learn this week that faith is shown in the celebrated victor as well as the unnamed sufferer. It's displayed in the parting of the Red Sea and the taking of a life through stones. Just when we think we might just be figuring out this faith-walk-thing, we're thrown a curve ball.

Nothing has changed in our definition of faith. It's still drawing near to God, regardless of where that might lead. It's still living—and dying—with an eternal perspective. The difference is the physical outcome. Exhibiting actions of faith does not guarantee a glorious outcome (not in our earthly terms anyway). Living a life of faith does not secure a life of comfort, riches, and good health. In fact, many modern-day heroes of faith live with constant hunger, lingering disease, and impending danger.

The key to a better understanding and experience of biblical faith is to let go of our assumptions and expectations of where our obedience will lead us.

1. Spend a few moments in silence, asking God to show you any misplaced expectations of faith-filled living. As He reveals any to you, jot them down below, and offer up a prayer of surrender, giving up those expectations to God's plan.

2. Read through Hebrews 11:29–40, and then rewrite the passage in a way that helps you begin to digest these verses to see the main idea.

Our heroes of faith, both in Hebrews 11 and beyond, are simply people. They are ordinary men and women who have been chosen by God to do great things for the sake of His glory. Some stop the mouths of lions, while others wander in destitution. Some He chose to become mighty warriors, others were appointed to suffer greatly. You and I can be heroes, too. Models of Christlike faith to our family, co-workers, and neighbors. God has placed you and me in the exact region and place in history for His purpose.

Some women today grow up as an "untouchable" in the slums of India, while I get to enjoy the comforts and freedom of modern-day America. Yet His purpose for each of us is the same: we are here to bring Him glory in the society we find ourselves in. With a confidence that God is always with us, regardless of how hard the journey is, we can join with Paul to say, "I can do all things"—whether that may be suffering or success—solely by His strength.

> For I have learned in whatever situation I am to be content.
> I know how to be brought low, and I know how to abound.
> In any and every circumstance, I have learned the secret of
> facing plenty and hunger, abundance and need. I can do all
> things through him who strengthens me.
>
> —PHILIPPIANS 4:11–13

(For more teaching on how to experience peace in any circumstance, check out my study *Everyday Peace*.)

> God, I don't always understand Your ways. Help me to see
> that You are always working—in both the easy and hard
> times. You are in control. I am not forgotten. By Your grace, I
> choose to have faith in your good and sovereign character, no
> matter what comes my way.

⁃!⁃ BONUS STUDY ⁃!⁃

Read Hebrews 11:29–40 again, and fill out the following chart with each character who showed faith and what action they took (if recorded) that was commended as faithful.

REFERENCE	CHARACTER (WHO EXHIBITED FAITH?)	ACTIONS TAKEN (BY FAITH, THEY DID WHAT?)

BONUS STUDY CHEAT SHEET

REFERENCE	CHARACTER (WHO EXHIBITED FAITH?)	ACTIONS TAKEN (BY FAITH, THEY DID WHAT?)
11:29	Israelites	Crossed Red Sea
11:30	Israelites	Saw Walls of Jericho Fall
11:31	Rahab	Welcomed Spies
11:32	Gideon	
11:32	Barak	
11:32	Samson	
11:32	Jephthah	
11:32	David	
11:32	Samuel	
11:32	Prophets	
11:35	Women	Received Back Their Dead By Resurrection
11:35b-38	The Nameless Faithful	Tortured, Refusing Release
		Suffered Mocking and Flogging
		Suffered Chains and Imprisonment
		Stoned
		Sawn in Two
		Killed with the Sword
		Clothed with Skins of Sheep and Goats
		Destitute, Afflicted, Mistreated
		Wandering in Deserts, Mountains, Dens, Caves

Observation

FOCUSing ON HEBREWS 11:29–40

So if it seems that there are going to be some temporary losses when you run this race with Jesus, you are right. That is why Jesus said to count the cost (Luke 14:25–33) before you sign on. But the marathon of the Christian life is not mainly loss. It is mainly gain. "For the joy that was set before him he endured the cross." It is only a matter of timing. If you see things with the eyes of God, there is a vapor's breath of loss and pain, and then everlasting joy (2 Corinthians 4:17).

—JOHN PIPER, from his sermon,

"Running With the Witnesses"

ALL OF OUR friends in Hebrews 11 have at least two things in common. First, they displayed faith in God while on this earth; there was fruit in their lives that pointed to a saving-faith relationship with their Creator, and that faith was credited to them as righteousness. By God's grace, they would spend eternity with God, through faith. Second, they all were promised deliverance. A better homeland, an imperishable inheritance, and great reward. They each held fast to a great hope of good things to come.

We too have been promised rescue. Deliverance always occurs, but it is not always as we think it should be. Too often the prayers spoken from discomfort, heartbreak, or tragedy are for the removal of pain and difficulties. Yet, the very presence of pain and difficulty is an opportunity for us to have faith in good things to come. Eternity. Our new home. The unfiltered presence of God.

No pain. No sorrow. No disappointment.

Sometimes, God provides earthly healing from cancer. Other times His provision is a complete healing—through physical death—and an eternal wholeness in His presence. God may deliver your soul from an addiction in an instant or you may struggle daily with that lifelong thorn until you are rewarded with a new, heavenly body that wants for nothing but the glory of God. I don't pretend to understand the exact how or why behind the reason some see deliverance from ailments on this earth and others don't, but I do know that God's Word is clear that Jesus is our faithful Deliverer.

And my Deliverer is coming.

1. Ask God to open your eyes to the truths about faith and hardship in these verses. Commit to aligning your beliefs to what His Word teaches about faith.

2. Up to this point in our studies, the actions of faith shown have predominantly happy endings. In this week's passage, we see a remarkable division where the outcomes listed are no longer ones often wished for. As you read Hebrews 11:29–40 today, list out each record of faith in either the "desirable" or "undesirable" section.

DESIRABLE	UNDESIRABLE

DESIRABLE	UNDESIRABLE

3. Which of these "undesirable" outcomes would be the hardest for you to go through? Why?

God's will for us can oftentimes be a hard pill to swallow. I don't always understand why He allows pain and suffering to enter my world, but this I do know: nothing enters my life without purpose. Nothing.

God is constantly in control. God is all knowing. God is eternally good.

> *Faithful Lord, I know You are in control, all knowing, and good. Yet, when my circumstances collide with my convictions, it is easy for my faith to waver. Help my unbelief! Give me the grace to cling to You even when my world is turned upside down.*

⁖ BONUS STUDY ⁖

Study Hebrews 11:38–40 again, looking for statements of truth about these men and women (beyond their circumstances).

CHEAT SHEET

2. List out each record of faith in either the "desirable" or "undesirable" section.

DESIRABLE	UNDESIRABLE
• Crossing of the Red Sea, deliverance from the Egyptians (v. 29) • Walls of Jericho fell (v. 30) • Rahab welcomed the spies (v. 31) • Gideon, Barak, Samson, Jephthah, David, Samuel, the prophets; conquered kingdoms, enforced justice, obtained promises, stopped the mouths of lions, quenched the power of fire, escaped the edge of the sword, made strong out of weakness (vv. 32–34) • Women received back their dead (v. 35)	• Torture • Mocking • Flogging • Chains and imprisonment • Stoned • Sawn in two • Killed with the sword • Destitute • Afflicted • Mistreated • Wandering in deserts, mountains, dens, and caves

BONUS STUDY CHEAT SHEET

Study Hebrews 11:38–40 again, looking for statements of truth about these men and women (beyond their circumstances):

The world was not worthy of them

Commended through their faith

Did not receive what was promised

God had provided something better

They are not made perfect without us

Clarification

FOCUSing ON HEBREWS 11:29–40

He is no fool who gives what he cannot keep to gain that which he cannot lose.

—Jim Elliot

I HAVE A nagging fear that has haunted me for decades, yet I've only recently recognized the root of my source of anxiety. The fear that torments me most is that of being unremarkable. Forgettable. Insignificant. When I look back on the darkest and most stressful times in my life, most of them stem from this fear of being marked as a nothing. I long to be known, adored, and looked to as one who has "arrived" and succeeded.

The last portion of Hebrews 11 touches the core of this fear. You may have noticed in your studies so far something in common about each of the characters listed in the "undesirable outcome" category. The men and women at the end of our Hall of Faith are all nameless. They are unsung heroes. Though they did not receive the comforts or accolades of this earth—like many of us desire—they have received the eternal comfort of the presence of Christ, and the crown of life for eternity.

"Do not fear what you are about to suffer. Behold, the devil is about to throw some of you into prison, that you may be tested, and for ten days you will have tribulation. Be faithful unto death, and I will give you the crown of life" (Revelation 2:10).

1. Begin your time today with a prayer of confession. Be honest with God

about the places that haunt your soul. What do you fear most?
What do you desire more than Him? After a time of confession, thank Him for
His continual forgiveness and great grace.

As we move into our Greek study time, keep the truth of His grace close
to your heart.

UNCOVER THE ORIGINAL MEANING

Step 1: DECIDE which English word you would like to study.
To start today's Greek study, look for any potential key words in Hebrews
11:29–40. As you find any repeated words or words that seem important
to the passage, write them down below.

Step 2: DISCOVER the Greek word in an interlinear Bible.
Choose one word and find the original Greek word using your interlinear
Bible or online tool. Write that Greek word below.

Step 3: DEFINE that Greek word using a Greek lexicon.
Now, look up the Greek word you've uncovered in a lexicon and note the
following:

Lexicon discovery:
• Definition:
• Times used:
• Part of speech:
• Other ways it is translated:
• Any special notes:

135

2. Follow the previous steps to look up one more word. Here are a few words to choose from:

Better (v. 35)

Worthy (v. 38)

Perfect (v. 40)

Lexicon discovery:

• Definition:

• Times used:

• Part of speech:

• Other ways it is translated:

• Any special notes:

3. What discoveries did you make through your clarification study? Which word did you learn the most about?

The unnamed eventually received deliverance, but it was not until they looked fully into the face of Jesus and heard "well done, my good and faithful servant" (Matthew 25:21) did they receive their recognition. In faith, they walked through the paths we often pray to avoid, and in so doing, they received the greatest recognition King Jesus will give in eternity.

I struggle with this reality. I often want recognition now. The rewards of heaven seem distant and hard to grasp. My flesh continually craves attention and accolades, and if I allow my sinful desires to run unfettered, I can find myself using my days for my glory, instead of His. And,

I certainly do not typically pray for the chance to show God faithful through suffering.

Our deeds are fruit—proof of our salvation. The world was not worthy of the deeds of the afflicted, mistreated, and stoned of Hebrews 11. The faith-filled actions of the suffering set them apart from the rest of the world, and gave proof to all around them of what they treasured more than comfort, riches, and even their own life—the presence of God. May we be more like these unnamed heroes.

> *God, thank You for Your great mercy! I am desperate for Your grace. I know that You have started a great work in me, and that You are faithful to complete that work. Continue to make me desire You more than any sort of recognition or position this world can offer. Make my heart desire You alone.*

⁎ BONUS STUDY ⁎

Continue these Greek study steps through as many words as you have time for.

Lexicon discovery:
- Definition:
- Times used:
- Part of speech:
- Other ways it is translated:
- Any special notes:

CHEAT SHEET

Step 3: DEFINE that Greek word using a Greek Lexicon.

Better (v. 35): kreittōn

• Definition: better; stronger; good

• Times used: 15 (11 of which are in the Book of Hebrews)

• Part of speech: adjective

• Other ways it is translated: superior

• Any special notes: Strong's #2908

Worthy (v. 38): axios

• Definition: worthy; proper

• Times used: 41

• Part of speech: adjective

• Other ways it is translated: deserve, keeping, due, worth, advisable, right

• Any special notes: Strong's #514; "in keeping with or corresponding to
  what is expected;" used in Acts 26:20: "performing deeds in keeping with
  their repentance."

Perfect (v. 40): teleioō

• Definition: complete; finish

• Times used: 23

• Part of speech: verb

• Other ways it is translated: accomplish, finish, ended, fulfill, completed

• Any special notes: Strong's #5048

Utilization

FOCUSing ON HEBREWS 11:29–40

Therefore, since we are surrounded by so great a cloud of witnesses . . . looking to Jesus, the founder and perfecter of our faith, who for the joy that was set before him endured the cross, despising the shame, and is seated at the right hand of the throne of God.

—HEBREWS 12:1–2

WE ALL NEED heroes. Heroes inspire us to action. They give us reason to believe that we too can achieve some sort of greatness. We can meet our goals, accomplish our big tasks, and climb those mountains. However, it's important to make sure our heroes are pursuing the goals of God's glory. If our heroes are climbing the corporate ladder for their own gain, or trying to become the next TV or music star to the detriment of their family, our eyes are fixed on the wrong heroes. We must find heroes who, like Jesus, look more to the promised joy than the fleeting allurements of this world.

Though unlikely heroes, at least in the world's eyes, we get to take another look at the nameless heroes of Hebrews 11. Though not all can be referenced back to specific stories in the Old Testament, many of them can. Our cross-referencing work today will help us get to know some of these faith-filled characters.

1. Begin your time in the Bible in prayer, and ask God to lead as you follow the storylines of our unsung heroes.

DISCOVER THE CONNECTIONS

2. Read Hebrews 11:29–40 again. Fill out the cross-referencing chart to discover the names of the characters listed in our passage. Simply look up each cross-reference below and look for the name of each story. Depending on the amount of time you have today, you can read the full story, or just the key verse(s) for our chart.

REFERENCE	CROSS-REFERENCE	NAME OF THE NAMELESS
11:36 "chains and imprisonment"	Genesis 39:20 (full story: Genesis 39:1–20)	
11:36 "chains and imprisonment"	Jeremiah 20:2 (full story: Jeremiah 19:14–20:2)	
11:37 "they were stoned"	2 Chronicles 24:21 (full story: 2 Chronicles 24:20–22)	
11:37 "killed with the sword"	Jeremiah 26:20–23	
11:38 "wandering"	1 Kings 19:9 (full story: 1 Kings 19:1–10)	

3. Record anything about these characters that stands out to you:

I'm thankful that God sees all, don't you? There is nothing done in His name that goes unrecognized by Him. It may never be noticed or seen here on earth, but one day we will receive commendation for every act of faith, and it will be all for His glory.

> Holy Spirit, open my eyes to see the path God has chosen for me today. Help me to walk it with confidence in the strength You give for whatever is around the corner. Give me perspective to understand how much You have given me, and the grace to use it all—the difficult and the wonderful—for Your glory.

⁙ BONUS STUDY ⁙

Look up more of the nameless:

REFERENCE	CROSS-REFERENCE	NAME OF THE NAMELESS
11:36 "chains and imprisonment"	Jeremiah 37:15 (full story: Jeremiah 37:11–15)	
11:37 "they were stoned"	1 Kings 21:13 (full story: 1 Kings 21:1–16)	
11:37 "killed with the sword"	1 Kings 19:9–10 (full story: 1 Kings 19:1–10)	
11:38 "wandering"	1 Samuel 22:1	
11:38 "wandering"	1 Kings 18:3–4	

If you are looking for more, use your study Bible or online tool to look up cross-references from additional verses as done in previous weeks.

CHEAT SHEET AND BONUS STUDY CHEAT SHEET

REFERENCE	CROSS-REFERENCE	NAME OF THE NAMELESS
11:36 "chains and imprisonment"	Genesis 39:20 (full story: Genesis 39:1–20)	Joseph
11:36 "chains and imprisonment"	Jeremiah 20:2 (full story: Jeremiah 19:14–20:2)	Jeremiah
11:36 "chains and imprisonment"	Jeremiah 37:15 (full story: Jeremiah 37:11-15)	Jeremiah
11:37 "they were stoned"	1 Kings 21:13 (full story: 1 Kings 21:1–16)	Naboth
11:37 "they were stoned"	2 Chronicles 24:21 (full story: 2 Chronicles 24:20–22)	Zechariah
11:37 "killed with the sword"	1 Kings 19:9–10 (full story: 1 Kings 19:1–10)	Elijah and previous prophets of God
11:37 "killed with the sword"	Jeremiah 26:20–23	Uriah
11:38 "wandering"	1 Samuel 22:1	David
11:38 "wandering"	1 Kings 18:3–4	Obadiah
11:38 "wandering"	1 Kings 19:9 (full story: 1 Kings 19:1–10)	Elijah

Summation

FOCUSing ON HEBREWS 11:29–40

GOD HAS GIVEN me a better provision. The promise we are given is not health, wealth, or comfort. The promise is the eternal presence of God. In a world that celebrates fame and fortune more than faith, I am in desperate need for God's grace to overcome the temptation to follow the crowd.

A true and saving faith in God is oh-so-much-more than a blind leap into danger. Faith is walking into whatever path He chooses, and trusting in His character with every step. Faith is living as a sojourner, continually turning my affections toward God and all His promises. Most of all, faith is dependence on a Savior who has provided a way for me to draw near to a holy God.

I will mess this faith thing up. Again and again, I will choose the allurements of this world instead of His presence. I will forget where my true home is, and will put down roots into the comfortable soil of this earth. I will find my significance in the accolades of my misplaced heroes, instead of finding my treasure in all Christ has provided for me.

But just as I first came to Jesus—by grace, through faith—I come again today and again tomorrow and again every day for the rest of my life. By grace, through faith, I will draw near to God. Because the good news about Jesus was not just for a schoolgirl in her bedroom when she first saw her need for Christ. The gospel is for my everyday. I need Jesus just as much as I did in that moment of salvation. In fact, as I grow in the knowledge of who God is (and who I am not), I realize I need Jesus even more today than ever.

By faith I take my next breath, asking Him to be glorified whatever comes my way. By faith I run to Him when I mess up. By faith I suffer whatever hardship comes my way. By faith I choose to live with an eternal perspective. By faith I rely on the provision of Christ for my righteousness, knowing that through Jesus, God is pleased with me.

By everyday faith I draw near to the presence of God.

I pray you will, too.

1. What lays heavy on your heart today? Journal out your feelings and ask God to meet you in the hard places.

RESPOND TO GOD'S WORD

IDENTIFY: What's the main idea?

2. Write out the main idea of Hebrews 11:29–40.

3. Read a commentary or study Bible to see how your observations line up. As you search the commentaries, ask God to make clear the meaning of any passages that are fuzzy to you. Record any additional observations.

If you still have any lingering questions about this week's verse, ask a trusted pastor, mentor, or friend what they think about the verse, or enter the online discussion at BibleStudyHub.com.

MODIFY: How do my beliefs line up to this main idea?

Journal through the following questions:

4. How does your view of faith line up with what you've learned this week? Who are your heroes? Are they faith-filled individuals? Do you have any heroes who have suffered with faith?

5. How does your view of God line up with what you've learned this week? Do you believe that God is good, even when He allows you to encounter hardship?

6. Are there any difficult places in your life you feel you don't deserve? Any actions of faith you feel have gone "unrewarded"?

GLORIFY: In light of this main idea, how can I realign my life to best reflect God's glory?

> In this you rejoice, though now for a little while, if necessary, you have been grieved by various trials, so that the tested genuineness of your faith—more precious than gold that perishes though it is tested by fire—may be found to result in praise and glory and honor at the revelation of Jesus Christ.
>
> —1 PETER 1:6–7

7. How could believing the truths discovered in Hebrews 11:29–40 affect your everyday moments?

8. What adjustments can you make to glorify God in your attitudes and actions this week?

God, my heart is turned toward the things of this earth more that I would like. I confess the places of bitterness in my hard-ships. Give me a heart for Your glory above all else. Help me to see Your good purposes, even in the places where I suffer.

A Note from Katie

Thank you for taking this journey of faith with me. It is an honor, joy, and privilege to be able to lead you through the Word. I hope you have a better grasp on what everyday faith can look like in your own life as a result of this study. Our faithful God has provided a way for you and me to draw near to His presence. What a gift! Let's respond to His great gift of grace with obedience to Him and worship of Him in our every moment.

Appendix

Glossary of Bible Study Terms

Interlinear Bible: a translation where each English word is linked to its original Greek word. There are many free interlinear Bibles online, as well as great apps you can download to your phone or tablet. Check out KatieOrr.me/Resources for current links.

Concordance: a helpful list of words found in the original languages of the Bible (mainly Hebrew and Greek) and the verses where you can find them.

Cross-reference: a notation in a Bible verse that indicates there are other passages that contain similar material.

Footnote: a numerical notation that refers readers to the bottom of a page for additional information.

Commentary: a reference book written by experts that explains the Bible. A good commentary will give you historical background and language information that may not be obvious from the passage.

Greek: the language in which most of the New Testament was written.

Hebrew: the language in which most of the Old Testament was written

Structure and Books of the Bible

Books of the Law (also known as the Pentateuch)
- Genesis
- Exodus
- Leviticus
- Numbers
- Deuteronomy

Books of History
- Joshua
- Judges
- Ruth
- 1 Samuel
- 2 Samuel
- 1 Kings
- 2 Kings
- 1 Chronicles
- 2 Chronicles
- Ezra
- Nehemiah
- Esther

Wisdom Literature
- Job
- Psalms
- Proverbs
- Ecclesiastes
- Song of Songs

Major Prophets
- Isaiah
- Jeremiah
- Lamentations
- Ezekiel
- Daniel

Minor Prophets
- Hosea
- Joel
- Amos
- Obadiah
- Jonah
- Micah
- Nahum
- Habakkuk
- Zephaniah
- Haggai
- Zechariah
- Malachi

New Testament (First four together are known as "The Gospels")

    Matthew

    Mark

    Luke

    John

    Acts

Epistles (or Letters) by Paul

    Romans

    1 Corinthians

    2 Corinthians

    Galatians

    Ephesians

    Philippians

    Colossians

    1 Thessalonians

    2 Thessalonians

    1 Timothy

    2 Timothy

    Titus

    Philemon

General Epistles (Letters not by Paul)

    Hebrews

    James

    1 Peter

    2 Peter

    1 John

    2 John

    3 John

    Jude

Apocalyptic Writing

    Revelation

Major Themes of the Bible

Though many view Scripture as a patchwork of historical accounts, morality tales, and wisdom for daily living, the Bible is really only one story—the mind-blowing story of God's plan to rescue fallen humanity. This storyline flows through every single book, chapter, verse, and word of Scripture. It's crucial that we know the movements, or themes, of the grand storyline so we don't miss the point of the passage we are studying.

For example, I grew up hearing about the story of David's adulterous affair with the beautiful, but married, Bathsheba. I heard how he covered his misdeeds with a murderous plot to snuff out her husband. This story was usually punctuated with a moral that went something like this, "Don't take what isn't yours!" While it is indeed good practice to refrain from taking what isn't ours, there is a much bigger connection to the grand story that we will miss if we stop at a moral lesson. So what then is this grand story, and how can we recognize it?

The story falls into four main themes, or movements: creation, fall, redemption, and completion*.

CREATION

The Bible begins by describing the creative work of God. His masterwork and crowning achievement was the creation of people. God put the first couple, Adam and Eve, in absolute paradise and gave them everything they needed to thrive. The best part of this place, the Garden of Eden, was that God walked among His people. They knew Him and were known by Him. The Bible even says they walked around naked because they had

157

no concept of shame or guilt. (See Genesis 2:25.) Life was perfect, just like God had designed.

FALL

In the Garden, God provided everything for Adam and Eve. But He also gave them instructions for how to live and established boundaries for their protection. Eventually, the first family decided to cross the boundary, and break the one rule God commanded them to keep. This decision was the most fateful error in history. At that precise moment, paradise was lost. The connection people experienced with God vanished. Adam and Eve's act was not simply a mistake but outright rebellion against the sovereign creator of the universe. It was, in no uncertain terms, a declaration of war against God. Every aspect of creation was fractured in that moment. Because of their choice, Adam and Eve introduced death and disease to the world, but more importantly, put a chasm between mankind and God that neither Adam nor Eve nor any person could ever hope to cross. Ever since the fall, all people are born with a tendency to sin. Like moths to a light, we are drawn to sin, and like Adam and Eve, our sin pushes us further away from any hope of experiencing God. You see God cannot be good if he doesn't punish sin, but if we all receive the punishment our sin deserves we would all be cast away from Him forever.

REDEMPTION

Fortunately, God was not caught off guard when Adam and Eve rebelled. God knew they would and had a plan in place to fix what they had broken. This plan meant sending Jesus to earth. Even though Jesus was the rightful King of all creation, He came to earth in perfect humility. He walked the earth for more than 30 years experiencing everything you and I do. Jesus grew tired at the end of a long day. He got hungry when

He didn't eat. He felt the pain of losing loved ones, and the disappointment of betrayal from friends. He went through all of life like we do with one massive exception—He never sinned. Jesus never disobeyed God, not even once. Because He was without sin, He was the only one in history who could bridge the gap between God and us. However, redemption came at a steep price. Jesus was nailed to a wooden cross and left to die a criminal's death. While He hung on the Cross, God put the full weight of our sin upon Jesus. When the King of the universe died, He paid the penalty for our sin. God poured out His righteous anger toward our sin on the sinless One. After Jesus died, He was buried and many believed all hope was lost. However, Jesus did not stay dead—having defeated sin on the Cross, He was raised from death and is alive today!

COMPLETION

The final theme in the grand storyline of the Bible is completion, the end of the story. Now that Jesus has paid the penalty for our sin, we have hope of reconciliation with God. This is such tremendous news because reconciliation means we are forgiven of sin and given eternal life. Reconciliation means that God dwells with us again. Finally, we know Him and are known by Him. Completion for us means entering into reconciliation with God through the only means He provided. We can only experience reconciliation under God's rescue plan if we trust Jesus to pay for our sin, and demonstrate this by repenting, or turning away, from our sin. But God's rescue plan does not end with us. One day, Jesus will come back and ultimately fix every part of fallen creation. King Jesus will come back to rule over God's people, and again establish a paradise that is free from the effects of sin.

Let's return to the David and Bathsheba story for a moment and try to find our place. David was the greatest, most godly king in the history of the Old Testament, but even he was affected by the fall and had a sinful nature. This story points out that what we really need is not a more disciplined eye, but a total transformation. We need to be delivered from the effects of the fall. It also illustrates how we don't simply need a king who loves God, but we need a King who is God. Do you see how this story connects to the arc of the grand storyline? Just look at how much glorious truth we miss out on if we stop short at "don't take what isn't yours."

*For a more detailed discussion on these themes, refer to Part 1 and 2 of *The Explicit Gospel* by Matt Chandler (pages 21–175) or Chapter 2 of Mark Dever's *The Gospel and Personal Evangelism* (pages 31–44).

Understanding the Ceremonial Law

TENT/TABERNACLE

WHAT IT WAS: The Tabernacle, or Tent of Meeting, was a portable sanctuary that served as the location of God's dwelling place on earth before the Temple was built. Craftsmen built the Tabernacle during the period of the Exodus when the Israelites wandered in the wilderness after leaving Egypt and before entering the Promised Land. During the Israelite's desert wanderings, the Tabernacle was situated in the center of the encampment.

ITS IMPORTANCE: The Tabernacle was a portable place of worship for the Israelites, allowing it to be moved as the camp moved.

NEW TESTAMENT SIGNIFICANCE: In the New Testament, God's presence dwells in each Christian.

KEY PASSAGES: Exodus 26; Numbers 1:51; 2:17; 18:21–24

TEMPLE

WHAT IT WAS: A permanent building that was the center of Hebrew worship. The original Temple was built by Solomon in 960 BC and took the place of the Tabernacle. The Temple was destroyed in AD 70 and has not been rebuilt.

ITS IMPORTANCE: The Temple was the dwelling place of God's presence on earth. The Temple was also to be the place where people from all nations could come and experience the one true God.

NEW TESTAMENT SIGNIFICANCE: In the New Testament, God's presence dwells in each Christian.

KEY PASSAGES: 2 Samuel 7:2–16; 1 Kings 5; 6; 8; 1 Corinthians 6:19; Ephesians 2:9–22

HOLY OF HOLIES

WHAT IT WAS: The inner sanctuary of the Temple (and before that, the inner sanctuary of the Tabernacle) contained the Ark of the Covenant. This room was separated from the rest of the Temple (or Tabernacle) by a large curtain called the veil.

ITS IMPORTANCE: This was the location where the sacrifice for Israel's sin was to be made on the Day of Atonement. The penalty for entering this room in an inappropriate way was death.

NEW TESTAMENT SIGNIFICANCE: Immediately following Jesus' death, the curtain separating the Holy of Holies was torn from top to bottom. There is nothing separating believers from God's presence.

KEY PASSAGES: Leviticus 16; Matthew 27:50–51

PRIESTS

WHAT THEY WERE: Professional ministers who performed ceremonial tasks in the service of God. Priests could only come from the tribe of

Levi, and had to be a direct descendent of Aaron, the brother of Moses.

THEIR IMPORTANCE: Only priests could perform the tasks of ceremonial worship.

NEW TESTAMENT SIGNIFICANCE: All believers have direct access to God, and are themselves priests.

KEY PASSAGES: Leviticus 8–10; 1 Timothy 2:5; 1 Peter 2:4–9

HIGH PRIESTS

WHAT THEY WERE: The High Priest was the highest ranking priest in Hebrew culture.

THEIR IMPORTANCE: The High Priest was the only priest who could enter the Holy of Holies on the Day of Atonement.

NEW TESTAMENT SIGNIFICANCE: Jesus is the Great High Priest who made a once and final sacrifice for our sin.

KEY PASSAGES: Hebrews 4:14–16; 10:1–18

ATONEMENT

WHAT IT WAS: Atonement is the necessary action required to remove the penalty of sin. In the Old Testament, atonement for sin required the blood sacrifice of an unblemished animal. Once a year, on the Day of Atonement, the High Priest makes a sacrifice on behalf of all Israel. During that sacrifice, one ram is killed to cover Israel's sin, and another is led into the wilderness to remove Israel's sin.

ITS IMPORTANCE: Sin always requires the shedding of blood. When Adam and Eve sinned, their nakedness was made known. To cover them, God killed an animal. In order to cover the sin of an entire people, God instituted the ceremonial law and the Day of Atonement. Atonement enforces God's justice while maintaining His mercy.

NEW TESTAMENT SIGNIFICANCE: Jesus is the spotless lamb who both covers our sin and removes it from our lives. Jesus' death is the final atonement that will be made for the sin of mankind, and thus fulfills the ceremonial law.

KEY PASSAGES: Leviticus 16; Hebrews 10:1–18; 1 Peter 1:19

How to Do a Greek Word Study

Learning more about the language used in the original version of Scripture can be a helpful tool toward a better understanding of the author's original meaning and intention in writing.

STEP 1: DECIDE which English word you would like to study.

Do a quick read of your passage and note any potential keywords and/or repeated words. There is no right or wrong way to do this! Simply select a few words you would like to learn more about.

STEP 2: DISCOVER the Greek word in an interlinear Bible.

Using an interlinear Bible (see glossary), find the original Greek word for each instance of the word in the passage you are studying. There may be more than one Greek word present.

STEP 3: DEFINE the Greek word using a Greek lexicon.

Look up your Greek word (or words if you found more than one) in a Greek lexicon (see glossary).

Continue through these three steps for each word you would like to study.

The Good News

GOD LOVES YOU

You are known and deeply loved by a great, glorious, and personal God. This God hand-formed you for a purpose (Ephesians 2:10), He has called you by name (Isaiah 43:1) and you are of great worth to Him (Luke 12:6–7).

WE HAVE A SIN PROBLEM

We are all sinners and are all therefore separated from God (Romans 3:23; 6:23). Even the "smallest" of sins is a great offense to God. He is a righteous judge who will not be in the presence of sin, and cannot allow sin to go unpunished. Our natural tendency toward sin has left us in desperate need of rescue because God must deal with our sin.

JESUS IS THE ONLY SOLUTION

Since God's standard is perfection, and we have all fallen short of the mark, Jesus is the *only* answer to our sin problem (John 14:6). Jesus lived a life of perfect obedience to God. So when Jesus died on the Cross, He alone was able to pay the penalty of our sin. After His death, Jesus rose from the dead, defeating death, and providing the one way we could be reconciled to God (2 Corinthians 5:17–21). Jesus Christ is the only one who can save us from our sins.

WE MUST CHOOSE TO BELIEVE

Trusting Christ is our only part in the gospel. Specifically, the Bible requires us to have faith in what Christ has done on our behalf (Ephesians 2:8–9). This type of faith is not just belief in God. Many people grow up believing that God exists but never enter into the Christian faith. Faith that saves comes from a desperate heart. A heart that longs for Jesus—the only solution for their sin problem—to be first and foremost in their life. We demonstrate that we have this type of saving faith by turning away, or repenting, from our sin.

FOCUSed 15 Study Method

Apply this method to 2–10 verses a day, over a week's time, for a deep encounter with God through His Word, in as little as 15 minutes a day.

Foundation: Enjoy Every Word

Read and rewrite the passage—Summarize, draw pictures, sentence-diagram, or simply copy the passage. Do whatever helps you slow down and enjoy each word.

Observation: Look at the Details

Take notes on what you see—Write down what is true in this passage. Look for truths about the character of God, promises to cling to, or commands given.

Clarification: Uncover the Original Meaning

- Decide which English word to study.
- Discover the Hebrew word in an interlinear Bible.
- Define that Hebrew word using a Hebrew lexicon.

Utilization: Discover the Connections in Scripture

Cross-reference—Look up the references in each verse to view the threads and themes throughout the Bible.

Summation: Respond to God's Word

- Identify the main idea of each passage.
- Modify my beliefs to the truths found in this passage.
- Glorify God by aligning my life to reflect the truths I've discovered.

New Hope® Publishers is a division of WMU®, an international organization that challenges Christian believers to understand and be radically involved in God's mission. For more information about WMU, go to wmu.com. More information about New Hope books may be found at NewHopePublishers.com. New Hope books may be purchased at your local bookstore.

Use the QR reader on your
smartphone to visit us online at
NewHopePublishers.com

If you've been blessed by this book, we would like to hear your story.
The publisher and author welcome your comments and
suggestions at: newhopereader@wmu.org.

Also in the FOCUSed15 series

ISBN-13: 978-1-59669-462-0
N164102 · $11.99

Everyday Hope—an easy-to-use, four-week study—will help you discover how to hold fast to God's promises amidst feelings of hopelessness in as few as 15 minutes per day. Exploring the Scripture, you'll learn more about His promises as they apply to you now and in the days to come.

Designed for women who are pressed for time but crave depth from their Bible study, *Everyday Hope* offers a relevant and lasting approach for reading and understanding Scripture as you work through the FOCUS method each week:

F — Foundation: Enjoy Every Word
O — Observation: Look at the Details
C — Clarification: Uncover the Original Meaning
U — Utilization: Discover the Connections
S — Summation: Respond to God's Word

Make each minute of your valuable time count as you learn about His promises so you can hold fast to Him in the chaos of life.

For more information, visit NewHopePublishers.com
and preview a video of Katie as she walks readers
through the FOCUS study method!

Also in the FOCUSed15 series

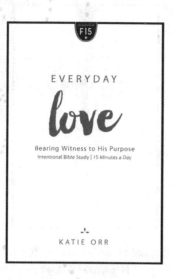

ISBN-13: 978-1-59669-463-7
N164103 · $11.99

What does Christian love look like in everyday moments?

Everyday Love—an easy-to-use, four-week study—helps you discover how your life can daily bear witness to God's purpose. Designed for women who are pressed for time but crave depth from their Bible study, *Everyday Love* utilizes the FOCUS method, which values quality over quantity and takes as few as 15 minutes a day.

This study guides you through 1 Corinthians 13 so you can find truths, promises, and commands; uncover word meanings; and discover your part in God's plan.

For more information, visit NewHopePublishers.com and preview a video of Katie as she walks readers through the FOCUS study method!

WorldCrafts^SM develops sustainable,
fair-trade businesses among impoverished
people around the world.

Each WorldCrafts product represents lives changed
by the opportunity to earn an income with
dignity and to hear the offer of everlasting life.

Visit NewHopePublishers.com/FOCUSed15
to shop WorldCrafts products related to the
FOCUSed15 Bible study series!

WORLDCRAFTS^SM
Committed. Holistic. Fair Trade.
WorldCrafts.org 1-800-968-7301

WorldCrafts℠ develops sustainable, fair-trade businesses among impoverished people around the world. Each WorldCrafts product represents lives changed by the opportunity to earn an income with dignity and to hear the offer of everlasting life.

Visit WorldCrafts.org to learn more about WorldCrafts artisans, hosting WorldCrafts parties and to shop!

WORLDCRAFTS℠

Committed. Holistic. Fair Trade.

WorldCrafts.org 1-800-968-7301

WorldCrafts is a division of WMU®.